Digital Signal Processing with MATLAB Manual

Written by

Md. Ariful Islam

Faculty Member

Dept. of Robotics & Mechatronics Engineering

University of Dhaka

Email: arif.rme@du.ac.bd

Educational Background:

B.Sc & M.Sc Engineering

Department of Electrical & Electronic Engineering

University of Dhaka

Email: arif_eeedu@yahoo.com

1st Edition: August 2022

CONTENTS

CHAPTER-1: DISCRETE TIME SYSTEM

1.1 Analog to Digital Signal

Problem-1: Conversion of analog sine wave signal to digital signal

Digital signal conversion theory:

The resolution is defined as

$$\Delta = \frac{x_{max} - x_{min}}{L - 1} = \frac{x_{max} - x_{min}}{2^n - 1}$$

MATLAB code:

```
clc; clear all; close all;
f=10; %range of the signal
n=3; %number of bits
q=f/(2^n-1); %Quantization
t=0:0.1:10;
y=abs(5*sin(t));
x0=fix(y/q); %Y = fix(X) rounds each element of X to the nearest integer toward zero. 1.9→ 1
y0=dec2bin(x0,n); %Convert from decimal to binary
y1=x0*q;
plot(t,y,'r')
hold on
plot(t,y1,'b')
hold off
```

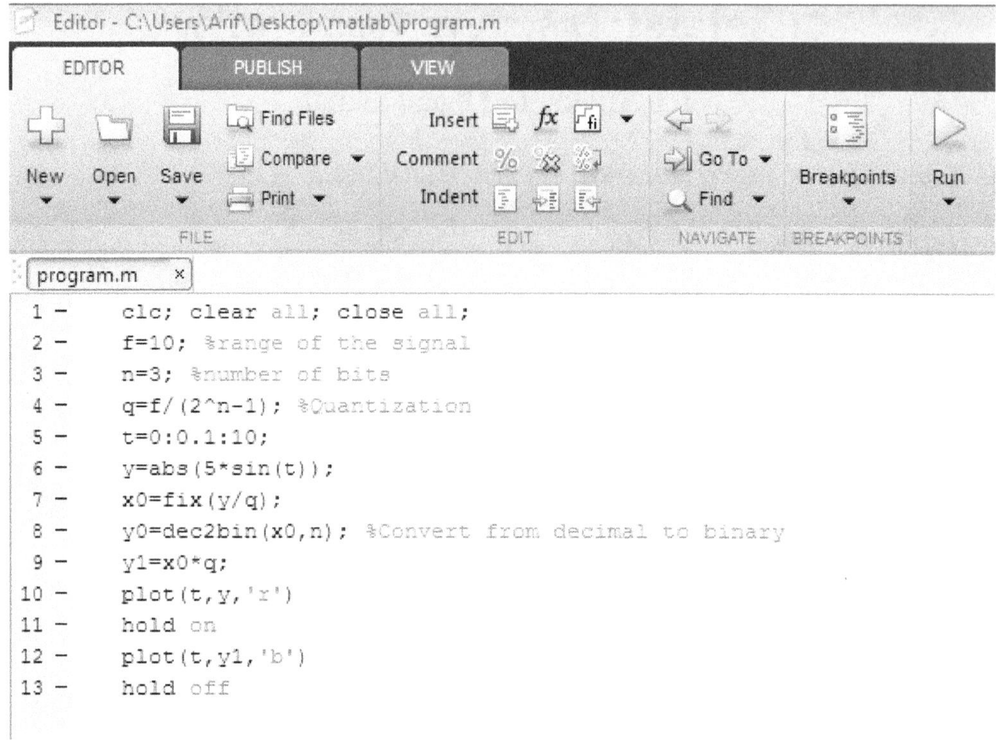


```matlab
clc; clear all; close all;
f=10; %range of the signal
n=3; %number of bits
q=f/(2^n-1); %Quantization
t=0:0.1:10;
y=abs(5*sin(t));
x0=fix(y/q);
y0=dec2bin(x0,n); %Convert from decimal to binary
y1=x0*q;
plot(t,y,'r')
hold on
plot(t,y1,'b')
hold off
```

If we run this program, the following output will be displayed. The red line indicates the analog signal and the blue line indicates the corresponding digital signal.

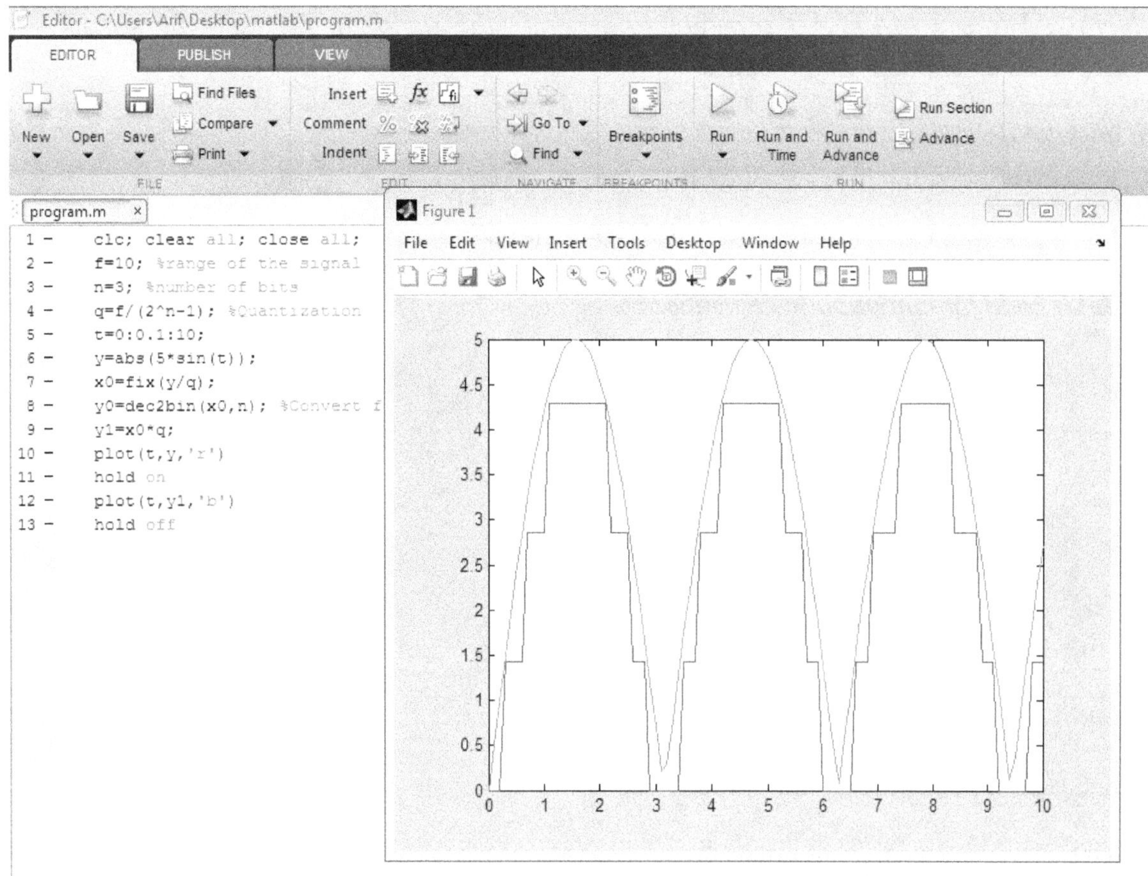

If we want to see the binary data, we have to type y0 in the command window.

1.2 Elementary signals generation

Problem-2: Write a MATLAB program to generate the standard discrete time signals – unit impulse, unit step and unit ramp signals.

Unit impulse definition:

$$\delta(n) = \begin{cases} 1 \ ; for \ n = 0 \\ 0 \ ; otherwise \end{cases}$$

MATLAB code for unit impulse generation:

n=[-20:1:20]; %specify the range of n

%********** Unit impulse signal

x1=1;

x2=0;

x=x1.*(n==0)+x2.*(n~=0); %generate unit impulse signal

subplot(3,1,1)

stem(n,x) %plot the generated unit impulse signal

xlabel('n');

ylabel('x(n)');

title('Unit impulse signal');

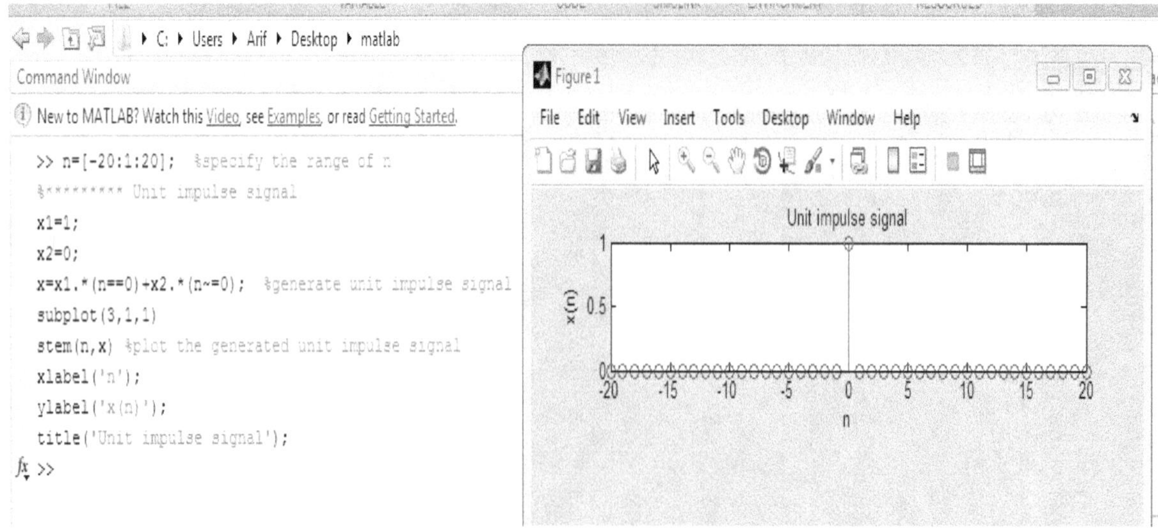

Unit step definition:

$$u(t) = \begin{cases} 1 \; ; for \; n \geq 0 \\ 0, \; for \; n < 0 \end{cases}$$

MATLAB code for unit step generation:

n=[-20:1:20]; %specify the range of n

%* * * * * * * * * Unit step signal

x1=1;

x2=0;

x=x1.*(n>=0)+x2.*(n<0); %generate unit step signal

subplot(3,1,2)

stem(n,x) %plot the generated unit step signal

xlabel('n');

ylabel('x(n)');

title('Unit step signal');

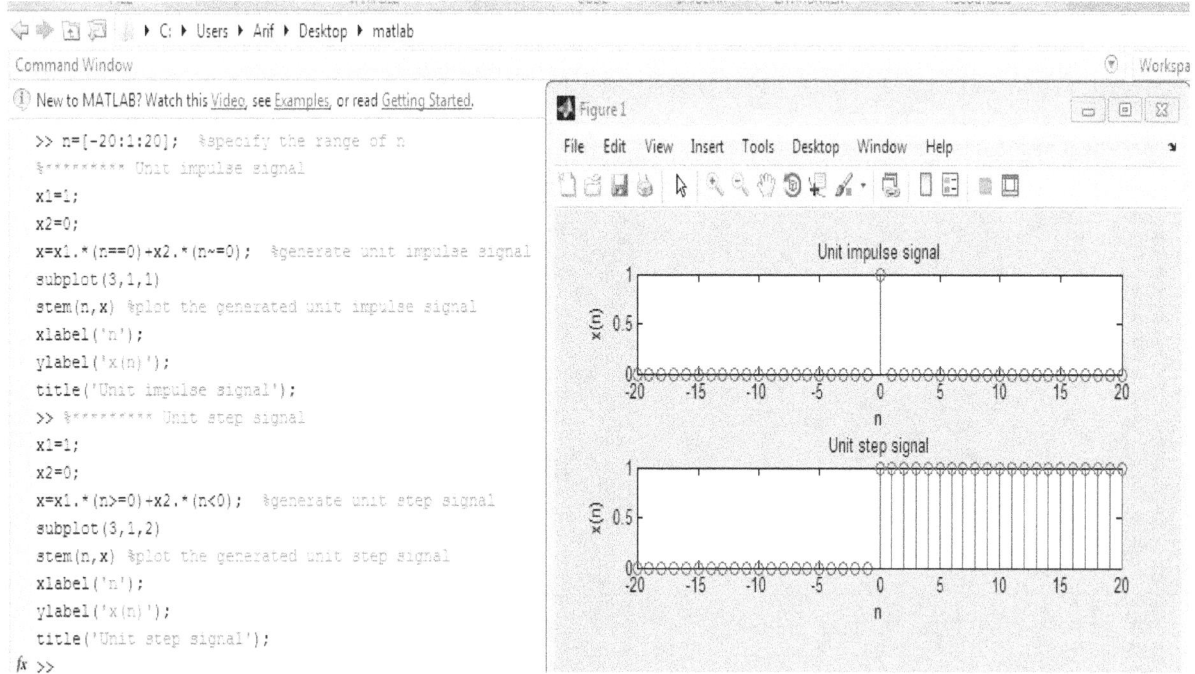

Unit ramp theory definition:

$$u_r(t) = \begin{cases} t \; ; for \; n \geq 0 \\ 0 \; ; for \; n < 0 \end{cases}$$

MATLAB code for unit ramp generation:

%********** Unit ramp signal

x1=n;

x2=0;

x=x1.*(n>=0)+x2.*(n<0); %generate unit ramp signal

subplot(3,1,3)

stem(n,x) %plot the generated unit ramp signal

xlabel('n');

ylabel('x(n)');

title('Unit ramp signal');

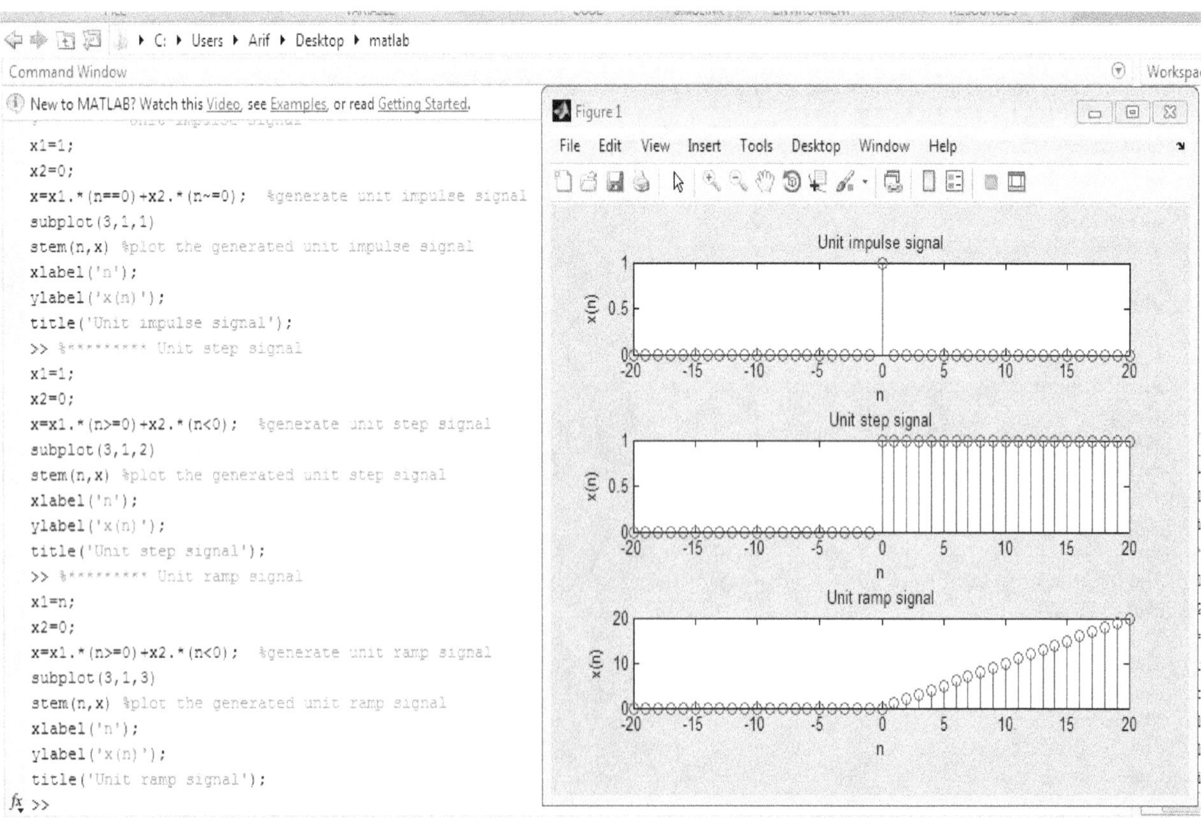

Problem-3: Write a MATLAB program to generate the standard discrete time signals – exponential and sinusoidal signals.

Exponential signal definition:

The real exponential signal is defined as

$$x(t) = Ae^{bt} \text{ ; Where, A and b are real}$$

When b is positive, the signal $x(t)$ will be an exponentially rising signal; and when b is negative, the signal $x(t)$ will be an exponentially decaying signal.

MATLAB code for Exponential signal generation:

n=[-20:1:20]; %specify the range of n

>> %****** Exponential Signal

>> A=0.95;

>> x=A.^n; %generate exponential signal

>> subplot(2,1,1); %plot generated exponential signal

>> stem(n,x);

>> xlabel('n');

>> ylabel('x(n)');

>> title('Exponential signal');

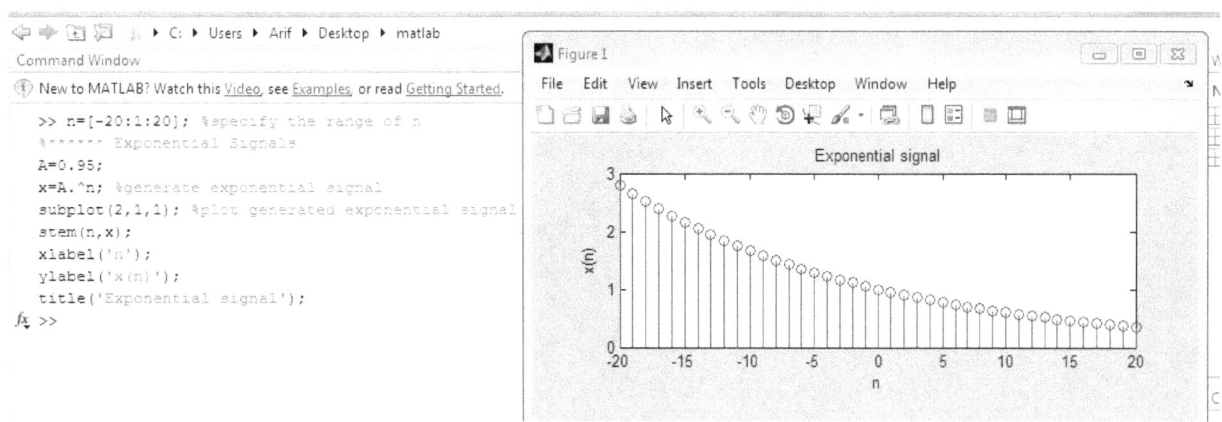

Sinusoidal signal definition:

The sinusoidal signal is defined as

$$x(t) = A sin(\omega t + \varphi)$$

Where, ω is the angular frequency in radian per second and $\omega = 2\pi f = \dfrac{2\pi}{T}$

f is the frequency in cycles per second or Hertz

T is the time interval in second

MATLAB code for sinusoidal signal generation:

```
%****** Sinusoidal Signals
 N=20; %Declare periodicity
f=1/20; %Compute frequency
x=sin(2*pi*f*n);
subplot(2,1,2); %plot generated sinusoidal signal
stem(n,x);
xlabel('n');
ylabel('x(n)');
title('Sinusoidal signal');
```

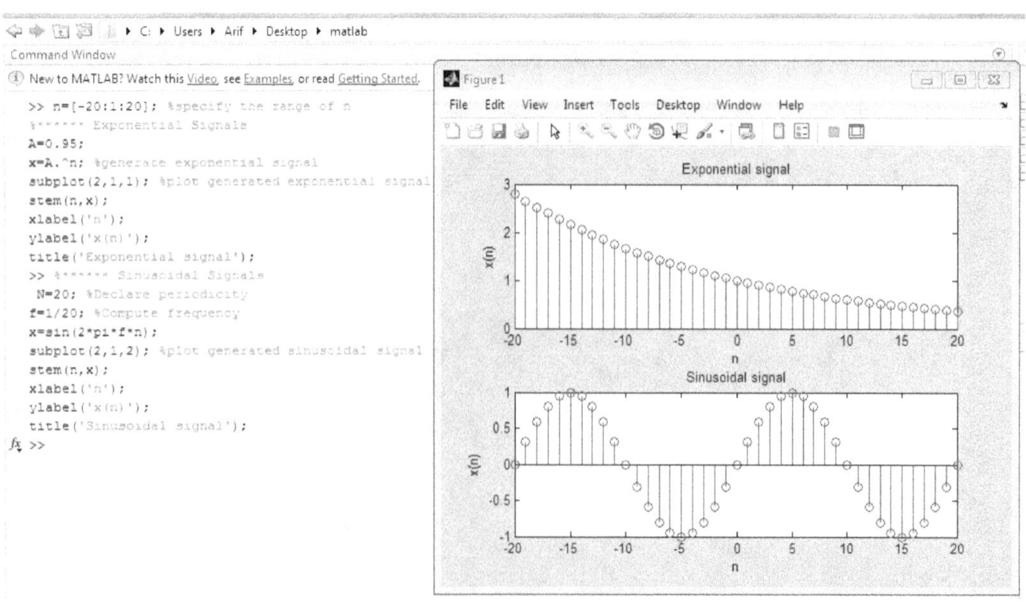

1.3 Even & Odd part of signals

Problem-4: Write a MATLAB program to find the even and odd part of the signal $x(n) = 0.8^n$

Theoretical framework:

Even signal definition: When a signal exhibits symmetry with respect to t=0, then it is called an even signal. The even signal will satisfy the condition, $x(-n) = x(n)$.

Even part: The event part $x_e(n)$ of signal $x(n)$ is defined as

$$x_e(n) = \frac{x(n) + x(-n)}{2}$$

Odd signal definition: When a signal exhibits antisymmetry with respect to t=0, then it is called an odd signal. The odd signal will satisfy the condition, $x(-n) = -x(n)$

Odd part: The odd part $x_o(t)$ of signal $x(n)$ is defined as

$$x_o(n) = \frac{x(n) - x(-n)}{2}$$

Folded Signal definition: The signal $x(n)$ that flips around $n = 0$ is called folded signal which is denoted by $x(-n)$.

MATLAB code for determining Even or Odd status:

```
n=[-5:1:5]; % Specify the range of n

A=0.8;

x1=A.^n; %Generate the given signal

x2=A.^(-n); % Generate the folded signal

if (x2==x1)

disp('Even signal');

else if (x2==(-x1))

disp('Odd signal');

else disp('Neither even nor Odd signal');

end

end
```

```
>> n=[-5:1:5]; % Specify the range of n
A=0.8;
x1=A.^n; %Generate the given signal
x2=A.^(-n); % Generate the folded signal
if (x2==x1)
disp('Even signal');
else if (x2==(-x1))
disp('Odd signal');
else disp('Neither even nor Odd signal');
end
end
Neither even nor Odd signal
fx >>
```

MATLAB code to compute even and odd part:

%Compute even and odd part

xe=(x1+x2)/2; %Compute even part

xo=(x1-x2)/2; %Compute odd part

subplot(2,2,1);

stem(n,x1);

xlabel('n');

ylabel('x1(n)');

title('signal x(n)');

subplot(2,2,2);

stem(n,x2);

xlabel('n');

ylabel('x2(n)');

title('signal x(-n)');

subplot(2,2,3);

stem(n,xe);

xlabel('n');

ylabel('xe(n)');

title('Even part of x(n)');

subplot(2,2,4);

stem(n,xo);

xlabel('n');

ylabel('xo(n)');

title('Odd part of x(n)');

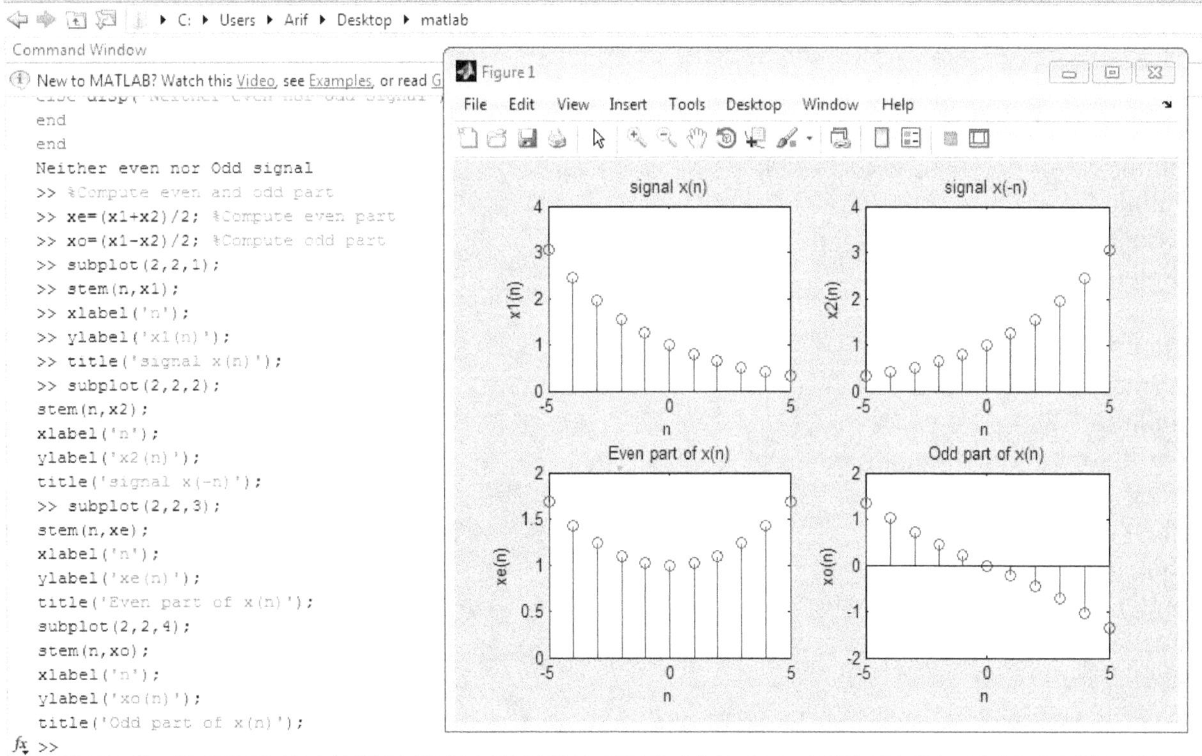

1.4 Linear Convolution

Problem-5(a): To perform linear convolution, write a MATLAB program in such a way that the impulse sequence and the input sequence of a linear time-invariant system will be taken by the user.

Convolution Theory:

Combining two signals to form a third signal that expresses how the shape of one is modified by the other.

$$y(n) = \sum_{k=-\infty}^{\infty} x(k)h(n-k)$$

Length of $y(n)$= Length of $x(n)$+Length of $h(n)$-1

MATLAB code for linear convolution:

```
%MATLAB program for linear convolution
clc;clear all; close all; %To generate only current result
x=input('Enter the input sequence: ');
h=input('Enter the impulse sequence: ');
y=conv(x,h); %Perform convolution
subplot(3,1,1);
stem(x) %plot input sequence
ylabel('Amplitude');
xlabel('Input sequence');
subplot(3,1,2);
stem(h) %plot impulse sequence
ylabel('Amplitude');
xlabel('Impulse sequence');
subplot(3,1,3);
stem(y) %plot the result of convolution
ylabel('Amplitude');
xlabel('Result of convolution');
disp('The resultant signal is shown in figure: ');
```

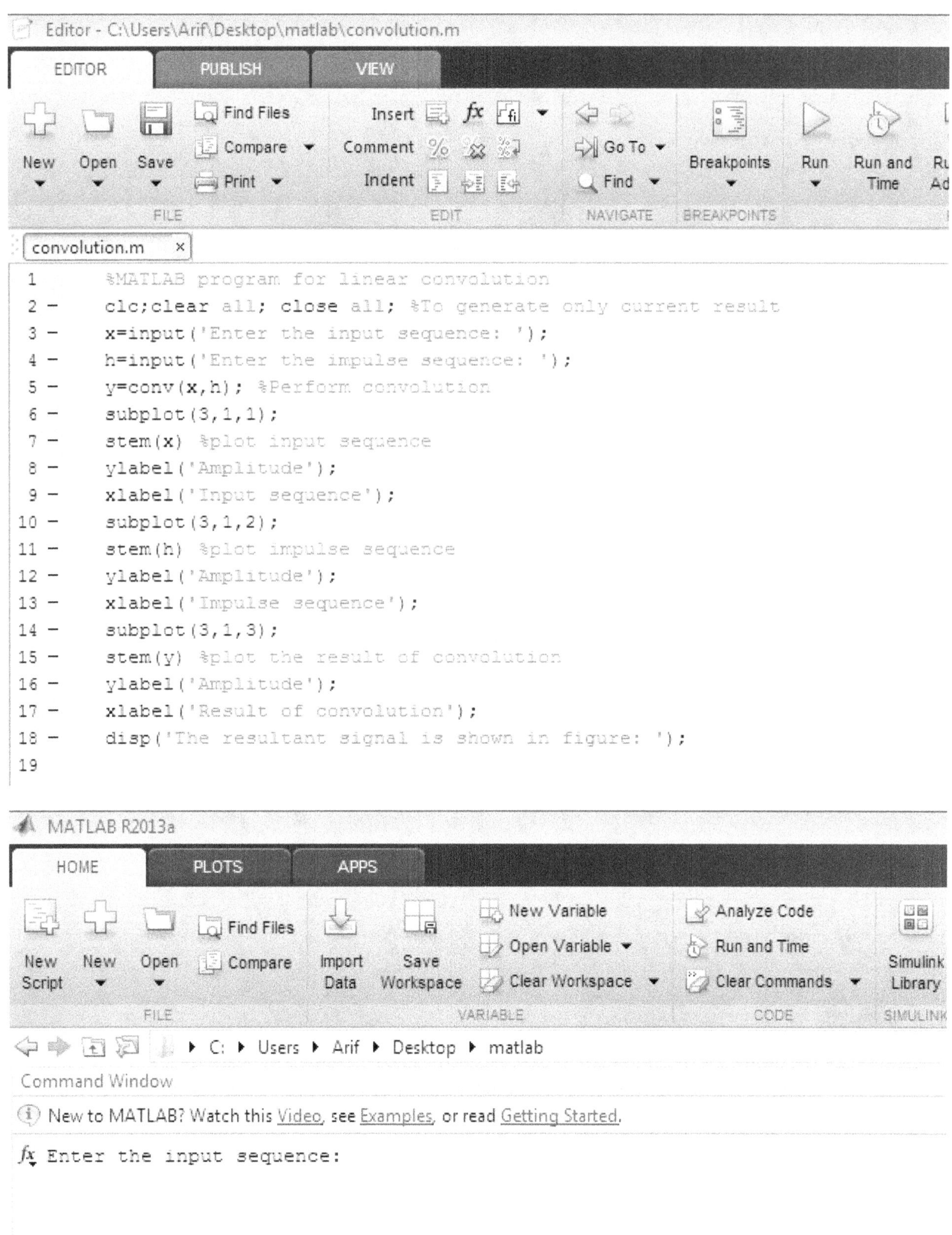


```matlab
1       %MATLAB program for linear convolution
2 -     clc;clear all; close all; %To generate only current result
3 -     x=input('Enter the input sequence: ');
4 -     h=input('Enter the impulse sequence: ');
5 -     y=conv(x,h); %Perform convolution
6 -     subplot(3,1,1);
7 -     stem(x) %plot input sequence
8 -     ylabel('Amplitude');
9 -     xlabel('Input sequence');
10 -    subplot(3,1,2);
11 -    stem(h) %plot impulse sequence
12 -    ylabel('Amplitude');
13 -    xlabel('Impulse sequence');
14 -    subplot(3,1,3);
15 -    stem(y) %plot the result of convolution
16 -    ylabel('Amplitude');
17 -    xlabel('Result of convolution');
18 -    disp('The resultant signal is shown in figure: ');
19
```

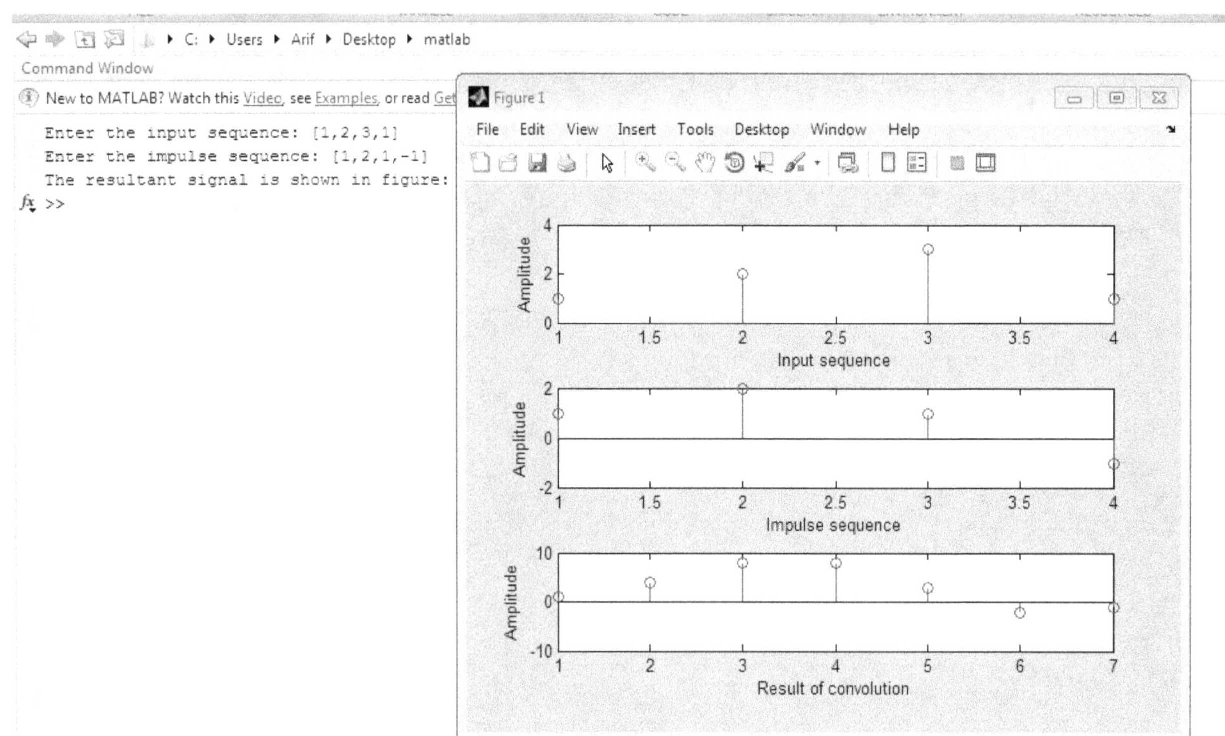

Problem-5(b): Write a MATLAB program to perform convolution of the following two discrete time signals.

$$x(n) = 1; 1 < n < 10$$

$$y(n) = 1; 2 < n < 10$$

MATLAB code:

```
%MATLAB program for convolution
clc;clear all; close all; %To generate only current result
n=0:1:15;
x=1.*(n>=1 & n<=10); %generation signal of x(n)
y=1.*(n>=2 & n<=10); %generation signal of y(n)
n1=length(x); %Find out the length of x(n)
n2=length(y); %Find out the length of y(n)
z=conv(x,y); %Perform convolution
n3=0:1:n1+n2-2; %specify range of n for z(n)
subplot(3,1,1);
stem(n,x) %plot x(n) sequence
ylabel('x(n)');
xlabel('n');
subplot(3,1,2);
stem(n,y) %plot y(n) sequence
```

```
ylabel('y(n)');
xlabel('n');
subplot(3,1,3);
stem(n3,z) %plot the result of convolution
ylabel('z(n)');
xlabel('n3');
```

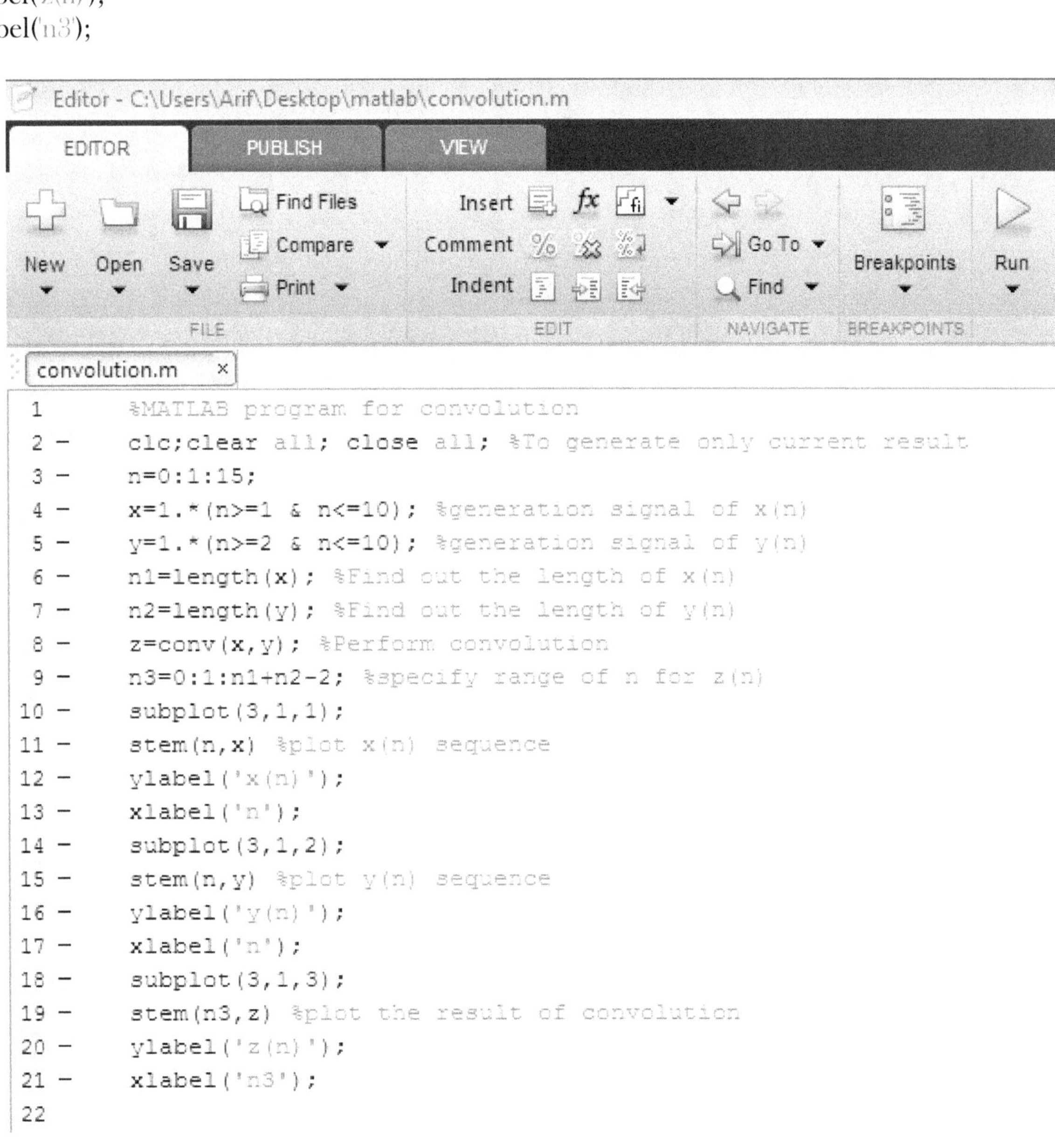

```
1    %MATLAB program for convolution
2 -  clc;clear all; close all; %To generate only current result
3 -  n=0:1:15;
4 -  x=1.*(n>=1 & n<=10); %generation signal of x(n)
5 -  y=1.*(n>=2 & n<=10); %generation signal of y(n)
6 -  n1=length(x); %Find out the length of x(n)
7 -  n2=length(y); %Find out the length of y(n)
8 -  z=conv(x,y); %Perform convolution
9 -  n3=0:1:n1+n2-2; %specify range of n for z(n)
10 - subplot(3,1,1);
11 - stem(n,x) %plot x(n) sequence
12 - ylabel('x(n)');
13 - xlabel('n');
14 - subplot(3,1,2);
15 - stem(n,y) %plot y(n) sequence
16 - ylabel('y(n)');
17 - xlabel('n');
18 - subplot(3,1,3);
19 - stem(n3,z) %plot the result of convolution
20 - ylabel('z(n)');
21 - xlabel('n3');
22
```

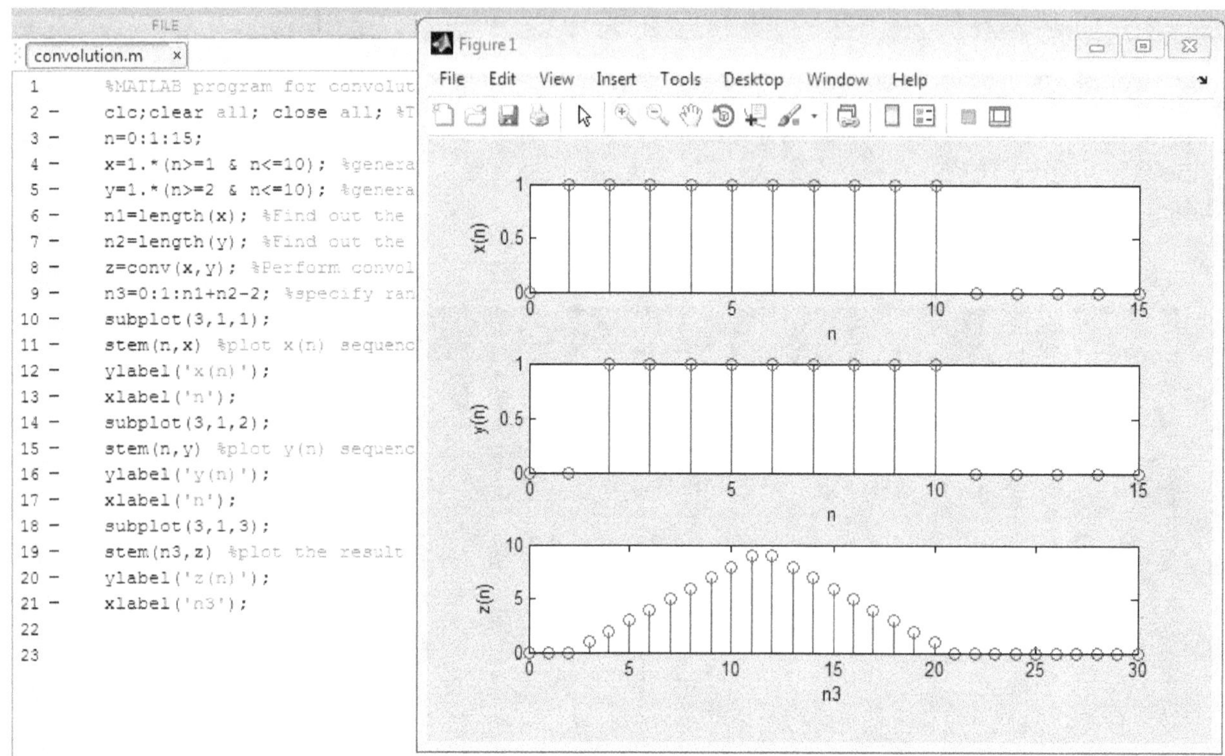

1.5 Cross-correlation

Problem-6: To perform cross correlation, write a MATLAB program in such a way that two input sequences will be taken by the user.

Correlation Theory:

Correlation is an operation that enables the measurement of the degree to which two sequences are similar. There are two types of correlation such as – Cross correlation and Auto correlation. The cross correlation is defined as

$$r_{xy}(I) = \sum_{n=-\infty}^{\infty} x(n)y(n-I)$$

Length of $r_{xy}(I)$ = Length of $x(n)$ + Length of $y(n)$ - 1

MATLAB code for cross correlation:

```
%MATLAB program for cross correlation
clc;clear all; close all; %To generate only current result
x=input('Enter the first sequence: ');
y=input('Enter the second sequence: ');
r=xcorr(x,y); %Perform cross correlation
subplot(3,1,1);
stem(x) %plot first sequence
```

```matlab
ylabel('Amplitude');
xlabel('First sequence');
subplot(3,1,2);
stem(y) %plot second sequence
ylabel('Amplitude');
xlabel('Second sequence');
subplot(3,1,3);
stem(r) %plot the result of cross correlation
ylabel('Amplitude');
xlabel('Result of cross correlation');
disp('The resultant signal is shown in figure: ');
```

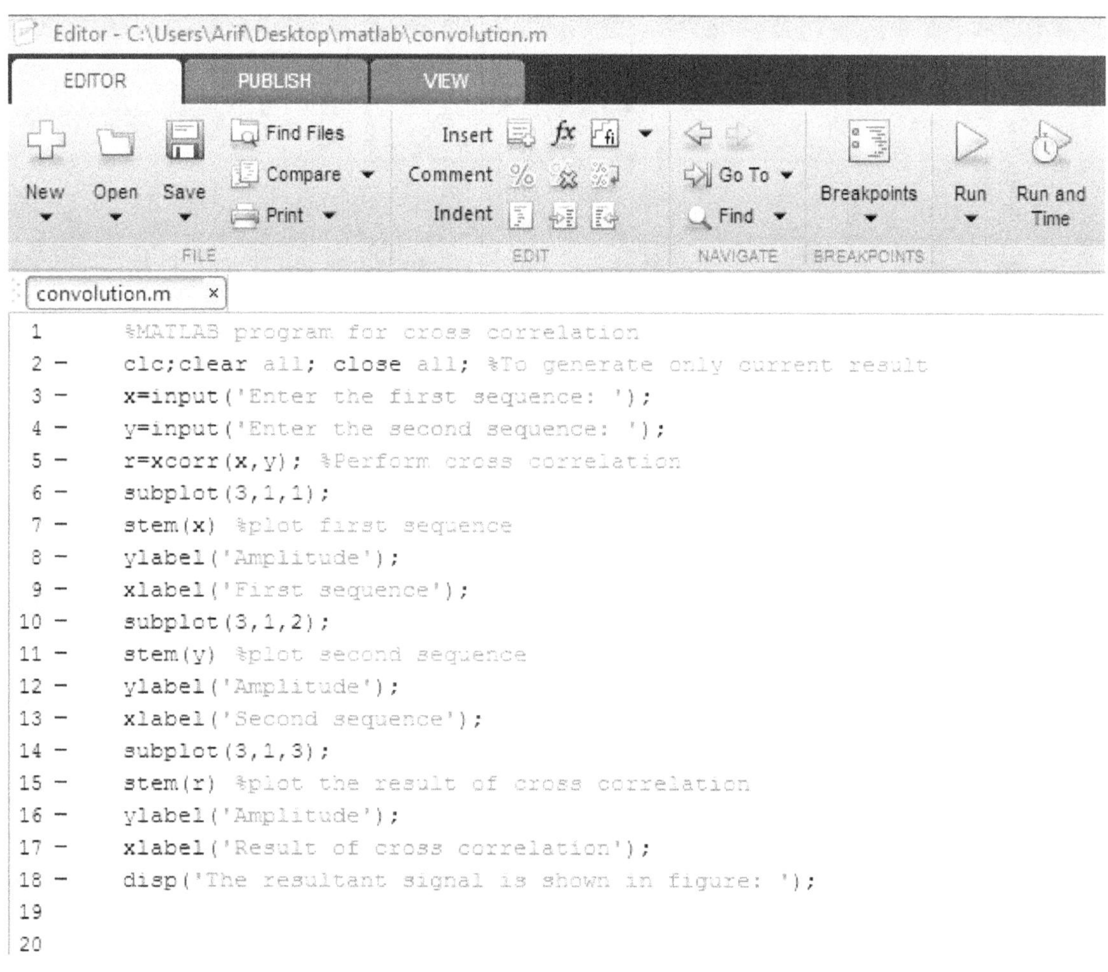

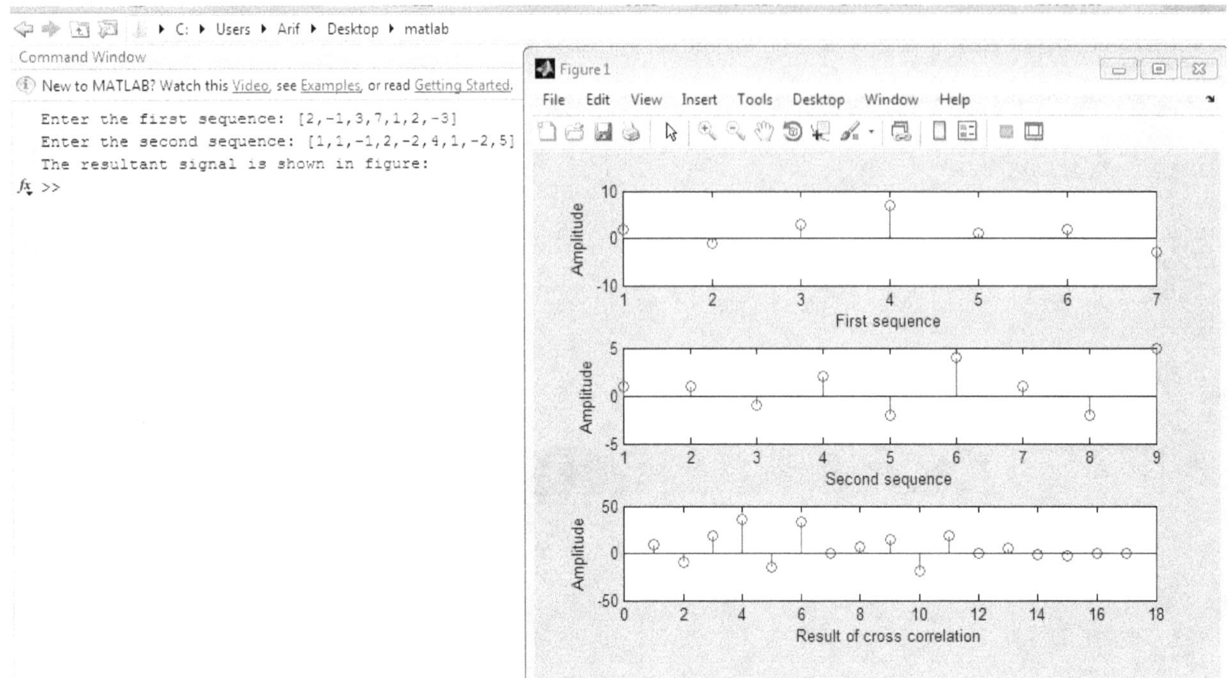

CHAPTER-2: Z-TRANSFORM

2.1 Z-Transform Theory

Z-Transform Theory:

Z-Transform is defined as

$$X(z) = \sum_{n=-\infty}^{\infty} x(n)z^{-n}$$

Problem-7(a): Write a MATLAB program to find the z-transform of the following causal signals.

$n, a^n, na^n, e^{-anT}, 0.5^n, 1 + n(0.4)^{n-1}$

MATLAB code for z-transform of $x(n) = n$

>> syms n T a real; %Let n,T,a be real variable

>> syms z complex; %Let z be complex variable

>> x=n;

>> disp('z-transform of "n" is: ');

>> ztrans(x)

```
>> syms n T a real; %Let n,T,a be real variable
>> syms z complex; %Let z be complex variable
>> x=n;
>> disp('z-transform of "n" is: ');
z-transform of "n" is:
>> ztrans(x)

ans =

z/(z - 1)^2
```

MATLAB code for z-transform of $x(n) = a^n$

>> syms n T a real; %Let n,T,a be real variable

>> syms z complex; %Let z be complex variable

>> x=a^n;

>> disp('z-transform of "a^n" is: ');

>> ztrans(x)

```
>> syms n T a real; %Let n,T,a be real variable
syms z complex; %Let z be complex variable
x=a^n;
disp('z-transform of "a^n" is: ');
ztrans(x)
z-transform of "a^n" is:

ans =

-z/(a - z)

fx >>
```

MATLAB code for z-transform of $x(n) = na^n$

>> syms n T a real; %Let n,T,a be real variable

>> syms z complex; %Let z be complex variable

>> x=n.*a^n;

>> disp('z-transform of "n*a^n" is: ');

>> ztrans(x)

```
>> syms n T a real; %Let n,T,a be real variable
syms z complex; %Let z be complex variable
x=n.*a^n;
disp('z-transform of "n*a^n" is: ');
ztrans(x)
z-transform of "n*a^n" is:

ans =

(a*z)/(a - z)^2

fx >>
```

MATLAB code for z-transform of $x(n) = e^{-anT}$

>> syms n T a real; %Let n,T,a be real variable

>> syms z complex; %Let z be complex variable

>> x=exp(-a*n*T);

>> disp('z-transform of " exp(-a*n*T)" is: ');

>> ztrans(x)

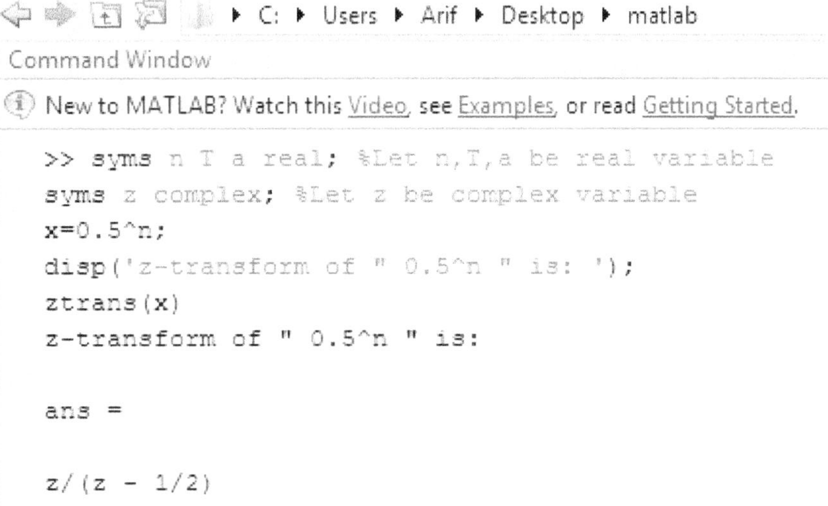

MATLAB code for z-transform of $x(n) = 0.5^n$

>> syms n T a real; %Let n,T,a be real variable

>> syms z complex; %Let z be complex variable

>> x=0.5^n;

>> disp('z-transform of " 0.5^n " is: ');

>> ztrans(x)

MATLAB code for z-transform of $x(n) = 1 + n(0.4)^{n-1}$

\>> syms n T a real; %Let n,T,a be real variable

\>> syms z complex; %Let z be complex variable

\>> x=1+n*(0.4^(n-1));

\>> disp('z-transform of " 1+n*(0.4^(n-1)) " is: ');

\>> ztrans(x)

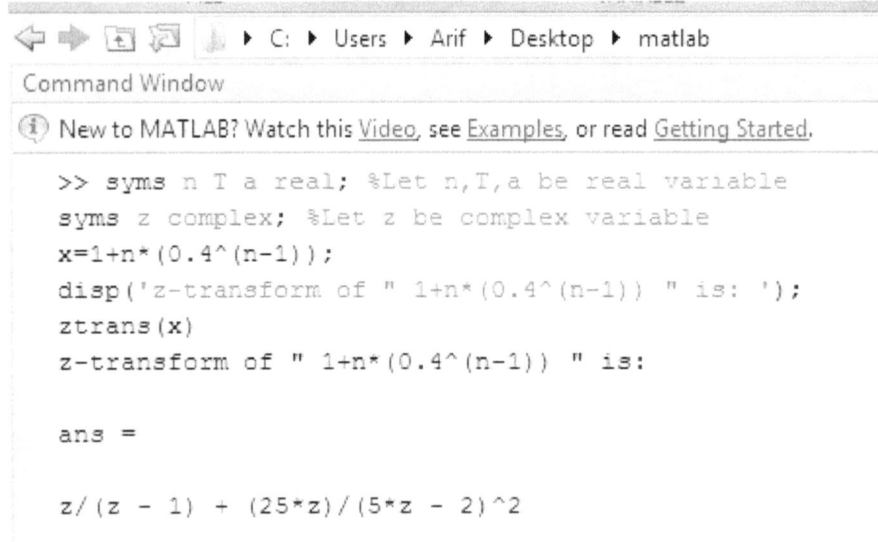

Problem-7(b): *Write a MATLAB program to find the inverse z-transform of the following z-domain signals.*

$$\frac{1}{(1 - 1.5z^{-1} + 0.5z^{-2})}, \; \frac{1}{(1 + z^{-1})(1 - z^{-1})^2}$$

MATLAB code for z-transform of $\dfrac{1}{(1 - 1.5z^{-1} + 0.5z^{-2})}$

\>> syms n real; %Let n be real variable

\>> syms z complex; %Let z be complex variable

\>> x=1/(1-1.5*(z^(-1))+0.5*(z^(-2)));

\>> disp('The inverse z-transform of " 1/(1-1.5*(z^(-1))+0.5*(z^(-2)))" is: ');

\>> iztrans(x)

C: ▸ Users ▸ Arif ▸ Desktop ▸ matlab

Command Window

New to MATLAB? Watch this Video, see Examples, or read Getting Started.

```
>> syms n real; %Let n be real variable
syms z complex; %Let z be complex variable
x=1/(1-1.5*(z^(-1))+0.5*(z^(-2)));
disp('The inverse z-transform of " 1/(1-1.5*(z^(-1))+0.5*(z^(-2)))" is: ');
iztrans(x)
The inverse z-transform of " 1/(1-1.5*(z^(-1))+0.5*(z^(-2)))" is:

ans =

2 - (1/2)^n
```

MATLAB code for z-transform of $\frac{1}{(1+z^{-1})(1-z^{-1})^2}$

>> syms n real; %Let n be real variable

>> syms z complex; %Let z be complex variable

>> x=1/((1+(z^(-1)))*((1-(z^(-1))^2)));

>> disp('The inverse z-transform of " 1/((1+(z^(-1)))*((1-(z^(-1))^2)))" is: ');

>> iztrans(x)

C: ▸ Users ▸ Arif ▸ Desktop ▸ matlab

Command Window

New to MATLAB? Watch this Video, see Examples, or read Getting Started.

```
>> syms n real; %Let n be real variable
syms z complex; %Let z be complex variable
x=1/((1+(z^(-1)))*((1-(z^(-1))^2)));
disp('The inverse z-transform of " 1/((1+(z^(-1)))*((1-(z^(-1))^2)))" is: ');
iztrans(x)
The inverse z-transform of " 1/((1+(z^(-1)))*((1-(z^(-1))^2)))" is:

ans =

(5*(-1)^n)/4 + ((-1)^n*(n - 1))/2 + 1/4

fx >>
```

CHAPTER-3: DISCRETE FOURIER TRANSFORM

3.1 DFT operation

Problem-8: Write a MATLAB program to perform DFT and sketch the magnitude and phase spectrum.

MATLAB code for DFT:

```
clc; clear all; close all;
x=input('Enter the sequence: ');
N=length(x);
y=fft(x); %calculate DFT
k=0:N-1;
subplot(2,1,1)
stem(k,abs(y))
xlabel('k');
ylabel('|y|');
title('Magnitude plot')
subplot(2,1,2)
stem(k,angle(y))
xlabel('k');
ylabel('angle of y');
title('Phase plot')
```

```
1 -    clc; clear all; close all;
2 -    x=input('Enter the sequence: ');
3 -    N=length(x);
4 -    y=fft(x); %calculate DFT
5 -    k=0:N-1;
6 -    subplot(2,1,1)
7 -    stem(k,abs(y))
8 -    xlabel('k');
9 -    ylabel('|y|');
10 -   title('Magnitude plot')
11 -   subplot(2,1,2)
12 -   stem(k,angle(y))
13 -   xlabel('k');
14 -   ylabel('angle of y');
15 -   title('Phase plot')
16
```

```
  Enter the sequence: [0 1 2 3]
  >> y

  y =

     6.0000 + 0.0000i  -2.0000 + 2.0000i  -2.0000 + 0.0000i  -2.0000 - 2.0000i

fx >>
```

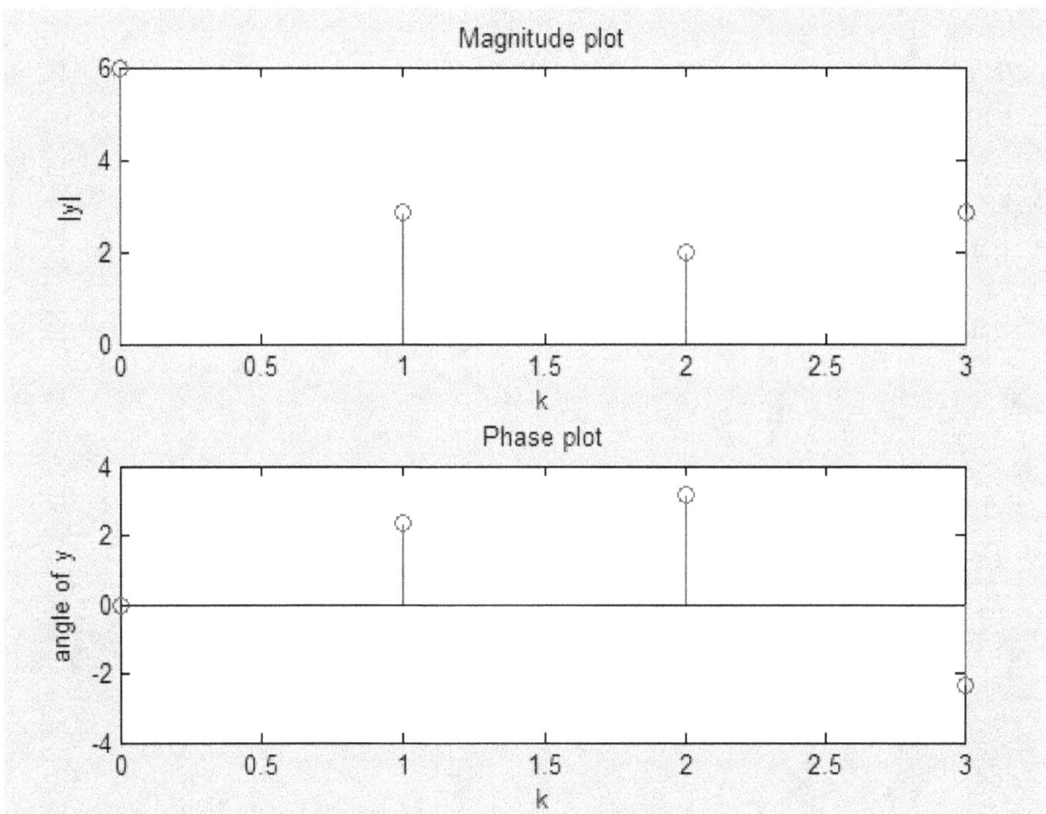

3.2 Circular Convolution using DFT

Problem-9: Write a program to perform circular convolution of the discrete time sequence $x(n) = \{2,1,2,1\}$ *and* $y(n) = \{1,2,3,4\}$ *using DFT.*

Circular convolution using DFT theory:

1. DFT of x(n)
2. DFT of y(n)
3. Product of 1 & 2
4. IDFT (Product of 1 & 2)

MATLAB code for circular convolution using DFT:

```
clc; clear all; close all;
N=4; %declare the value of N
x=[2,1,2,1]; %declare the input sequence
y=[1,2,3,4]; %declare the input sequence
 disp('The 4-point DFT of x(n) is: ');
x1=fft(x,N) %compute 4-point DFT of x(n)
 disp('The 4-point DFT of y(n) is: ');
y1=fft(y,N) %compute 4-point DFT of y(n)
 disp('The product of DFTs is: ');
z1=x1.*y1 %Product of DFTs
 disp('Circular convolution of x(n) and y(n) is: ');
z=ifft(z1) %Perform IDFT to get result of circular convolution
```

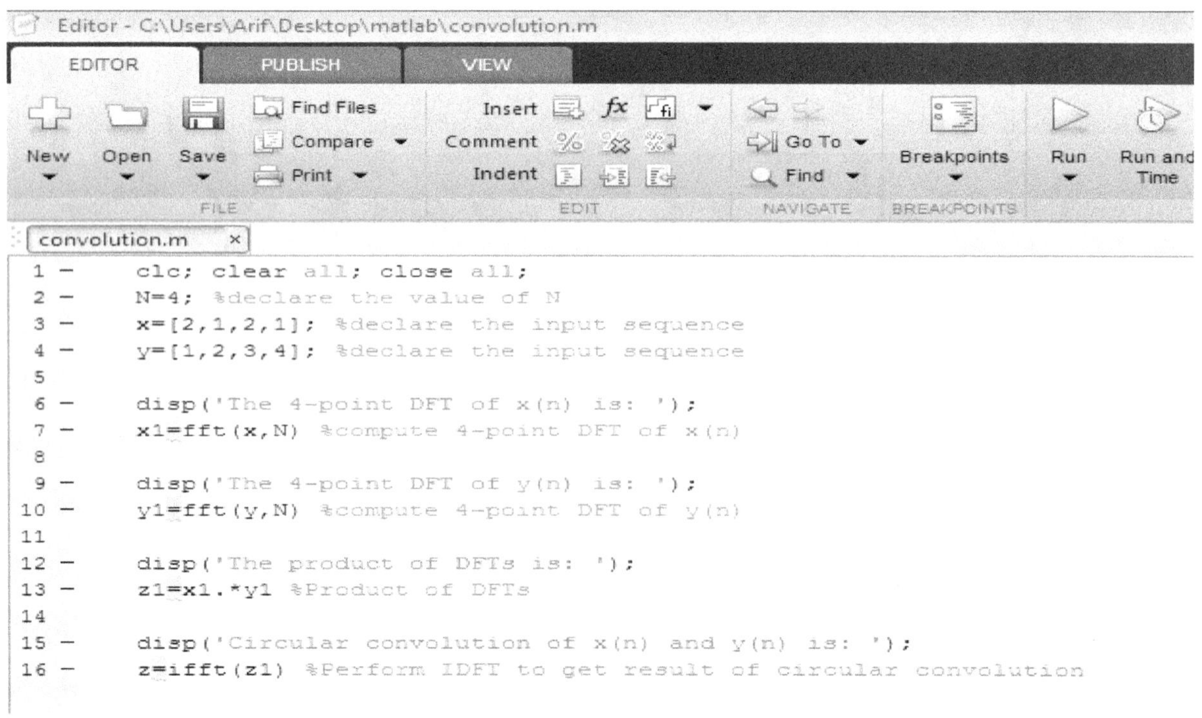

```
 1 -    clc; clear all; close all;
 2 -    N=4; %declare the value of N
 3 -    x=[2,1,2,1]; %declare the input sequence
 4 -    y=[1,2,3,4]; %declare the input sequence
 5
 6 -    disp('The 4-point DFT of x(n) is: ');
 7 -    x1=fft(x,N) %compute 4-point DFT of x(n)
 8
 9 -    disp('The 4-point DFT of y(n) is: ');
10 -    y1=fft(y,N) %compute 4-point DFT of y(n)
11
12 -    disp('The product of DFTs is: ');
13 -    z1=x1.*y1 %Product of DFTs
14
15 -    disp('Circular convolution of x(n) and y(n) is: ');
16 -    z=ifft(z1) %Perform IDFT to get result of circular convolution
```

```
◄� ➡ ⊞ ⊡    ▶  C: ▶ Users ▶ Arif ▶ Desktop ▶ matlab
Command Window
ⓘ New to MATLAB? Watch this Video, see Examples, or read Getting Started.
  The 4-point DFT of x(n) is:

  x1 =

       6      0     2      0

  The 4-point DFT of y(n) is:

  y1 =

    10.0000 + 0.0000i  -2.0000 + 2.0000i  -2.0000 + 0.0000i  -2.0000 - 2.0000i

  The product of DFTs is:

  z1 =

      60      0     -4      0

  Circular convolution of x(n) and y(n) is:

  z =

      14     16     14     16

fx >>
```

CHAPTER-4: DIGITAL FILTER IMPLEMENTATION

4.1 Filter Design using FDA Tools

Problem-10: Use MATLAB to design and analyze a low pass filter with the following specifications:

- *Passband attenuation 1 dB*
- *Stopband attenuation 80 dB*
- *A passband frequency 0.2 [Normalized (0 to 1)]*
- *A stopband frequency 0.5 [Normalized (0 to 1)]*

Use an FIR Equiripple filter.

Getting Started

Type fdatool at the MATLAB command prompt:

>>fdatool

A Tip of the Day dialog displays with suggestions for using Filter Designer. Then, the GUI displays with a default filter.

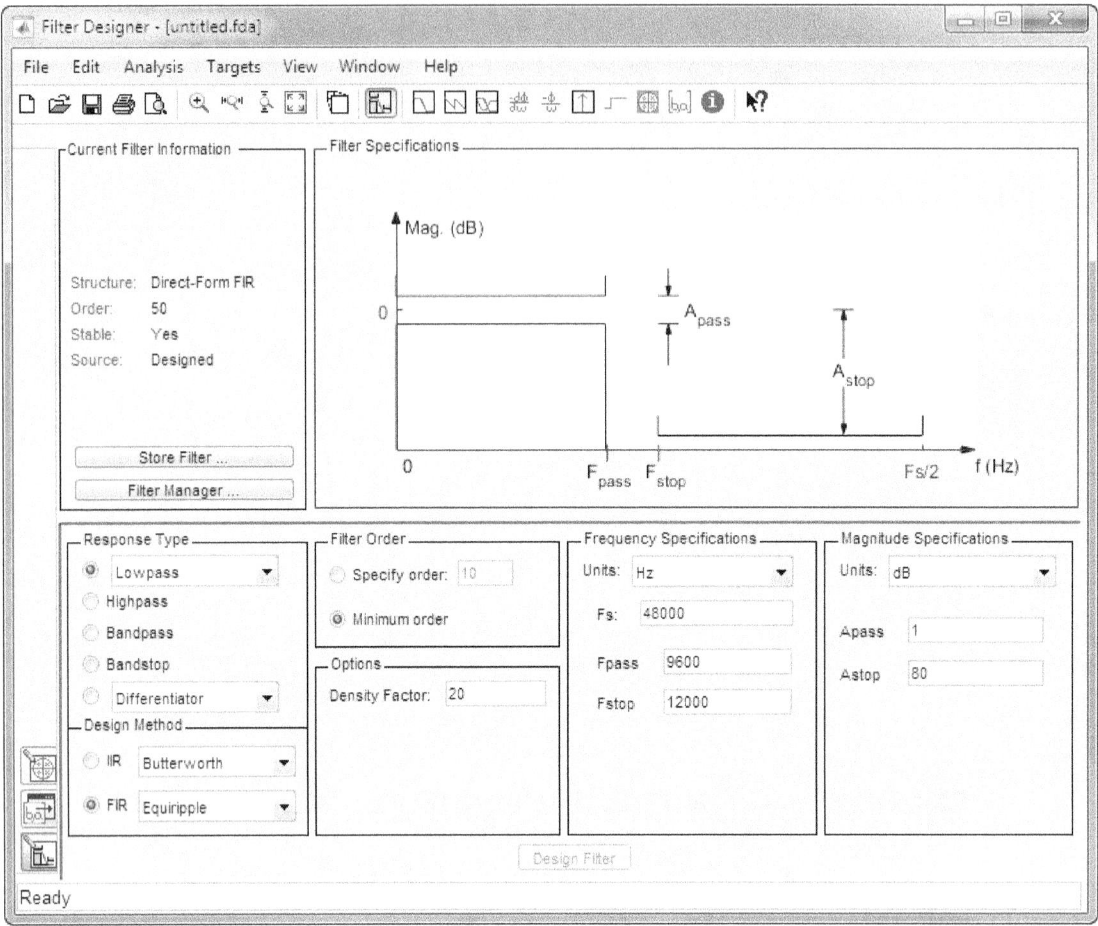

The GUI has three main regions:

- The Current Filter Information region
- The Filter Display region and
- The Design panel

The upper half of the GUI displays information on filter specifications and responses for the current filter. The Current Filter Information region, in the upper left, displays filter properties, namely the filter structure, order, number of sections used and whether the filter is stable or not. It also provides access to the Filter manager for working with multiple filters.

The Filter Display region, in the upper right, displays various filter responses, such as, magnitude response, group delay and filter coefficients.

The lower half of the GUI is the interactive portion of Filter Designer. The Design Panel, in the lower half is where you define your filter specifications. It controls what is displayed in the other two upper regions. Other panels can be displayed in the lower half by using the sidebar buttons.

The tool includes Context-sensitive help. You can right-click or click the *What's This?* button to get information on the different parts of the tool.

Designing a Filter

We will design a low pass filter that passes all frequencies less than or equal to 20% of the Nyquist frequency (half the sampling frequency) and attenuates frequencies greater than or equal to 50% of the Nyquist frequency. We will use an FIR Equiripple filter with these specifications:

- Passband attenuation 1 dB
- Stopband attenuation 80 dB
- A passband frequency 0.2 [Normalized (0 to 1)]
- A stopband frequency 0.5 [Normalized (0 to 1)]

To implement this design, we will use the following specifications:

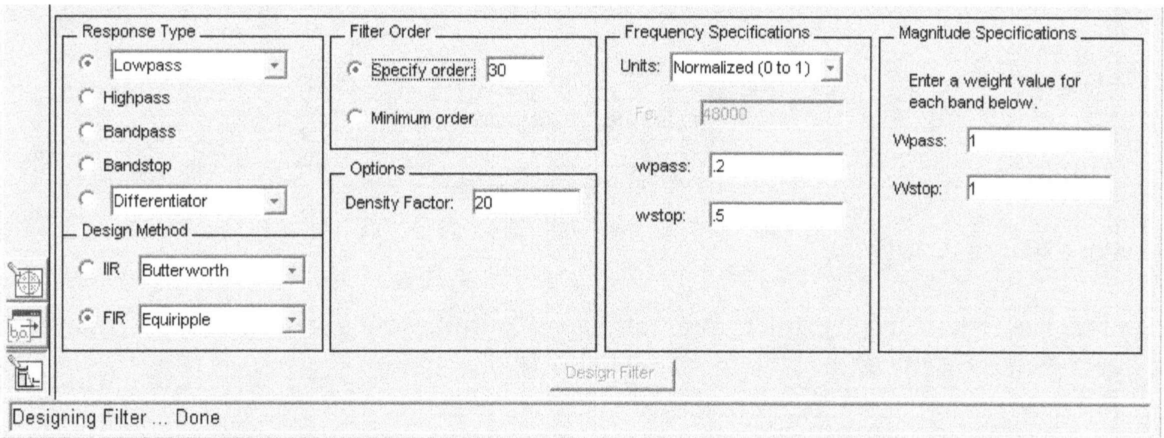

1. Select **Lowpass** from the dropdown menu under **Response Type** and **Equiripple** under **FIR Design Method**. In general, when you change the Response Type or Design Method, the filter parameters and Filter Display region update automatically.

2. Select **Specify order** in the **Filter Order** area and enter **30**.

3. The FIR Equiripple filter has a **Density Factor** option which controls the density of the frequency grid. Increasing the value creates a filter which more closely approximates an ideal equiripple filter, but more time is required as the computation increases. Leave this value at 20.

4. Select **Normalized (0 to 1)** in the Units pull down menu in the **Frequency Specifications** area.

5. Enter **0.2** for **wpass** and **0.5** for **wstop** in the **Frequency Specifications** area.

6. **Wpass** and **Wstop**, in the **Magnitude Specifications** area are positive weights, one per band, used during optimization in the FIR Equiripple filter. Leave these values at 1.

7. After setting the design specifications, click the **Design Filter** button at the bottom of the GUI to design the filter.

The magnitude response of the filter is displayed in the Filter Analysis area after the coefficients are computed.

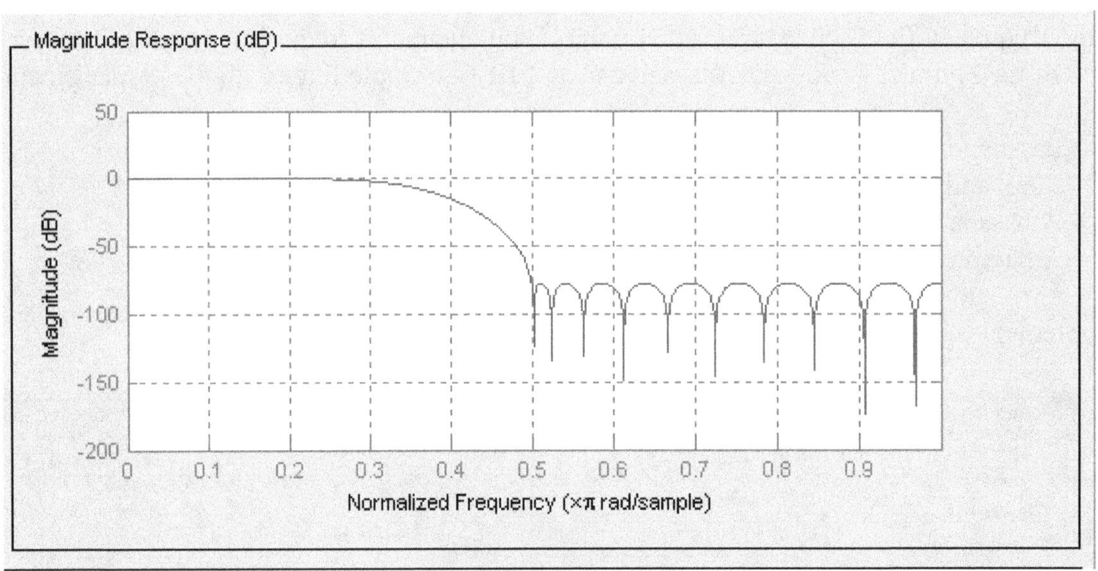

Viewing other Analyses

Once you have designed the filter, you can view the following filter analyses in the display window by clicking any of the buttons on the toolbar:

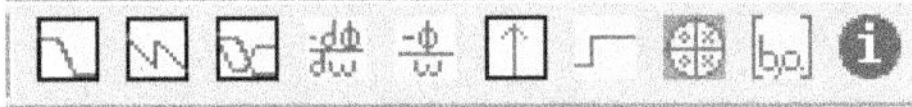

In order from left to right, the buttons are

- Magnitude response
- Phase response
- Magnitude and Phase responses
- Group delay response
- Phase delay response
- Impulse response
- Step response
- Pole-zero plot
- Filter Coefficients
- Filter Information

Comparing the Design to Filter Specifications

Filter Designer allows you to measure how closely your design meets the filter specifications by using Specification masks which overlay the filter specifications on the response plot. In the Display Region, when the Magnitude plot is displayed, right click on the y-axis label 'Magnitude (dB)' and select **Magnitude**. Then select **Specification Mask** from the **View** menu to overlay the filter specifications on the response plot.

The magnitude response of the filter with Specification mask is shown below:

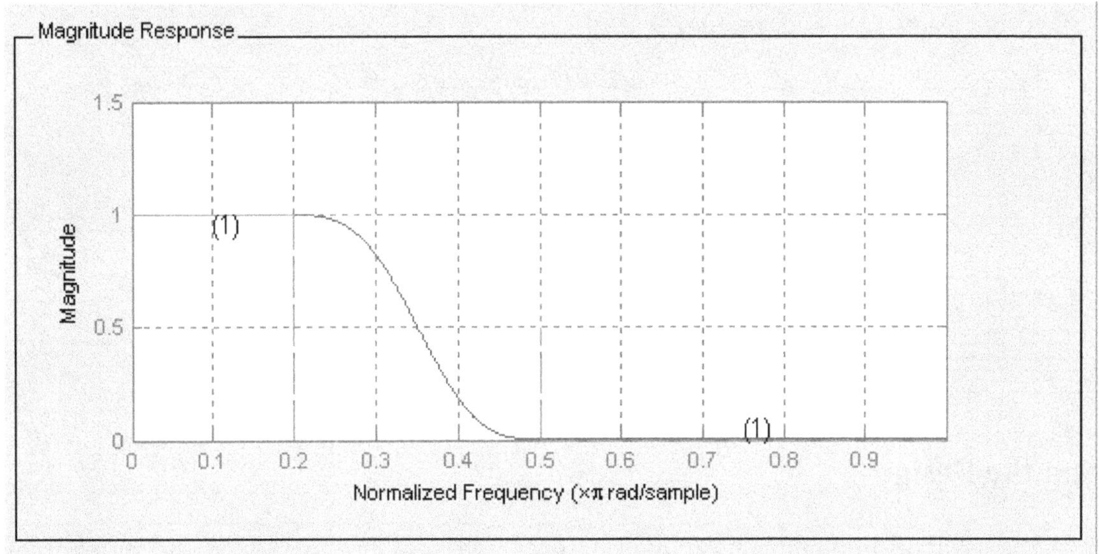

Changing Axes Units

You can change the x- or y-axis units by right-clicking the mouse on an axis label and selecting the desired units. The current units have a checkmark.

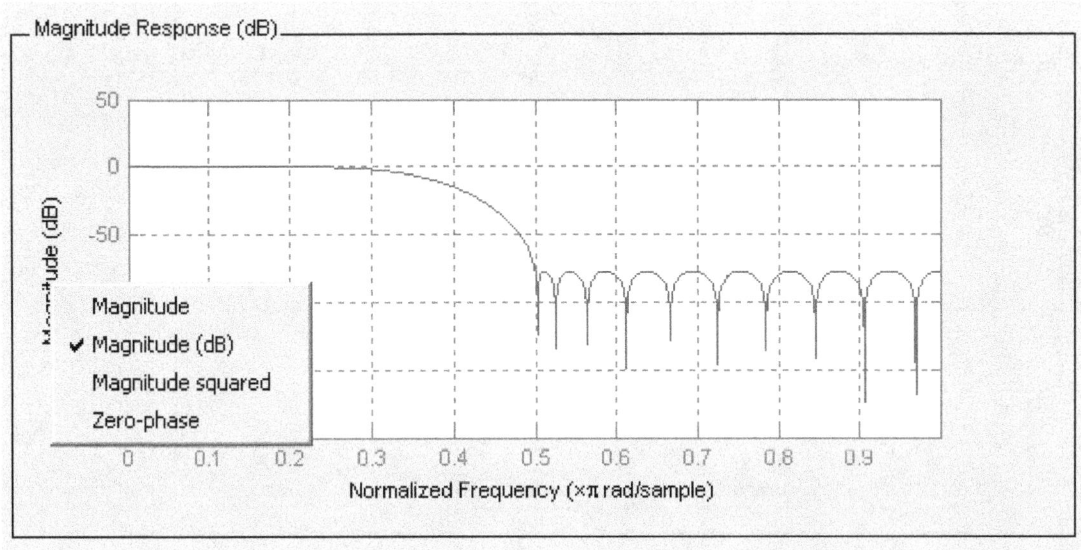

Marking Data Points

In the Display region, you can click on any point in the plot to add a data marker, which displays the values at that point. Right-clicking on the data marker displays a menu where you can move, delete or adjust the appearance of the data markers.

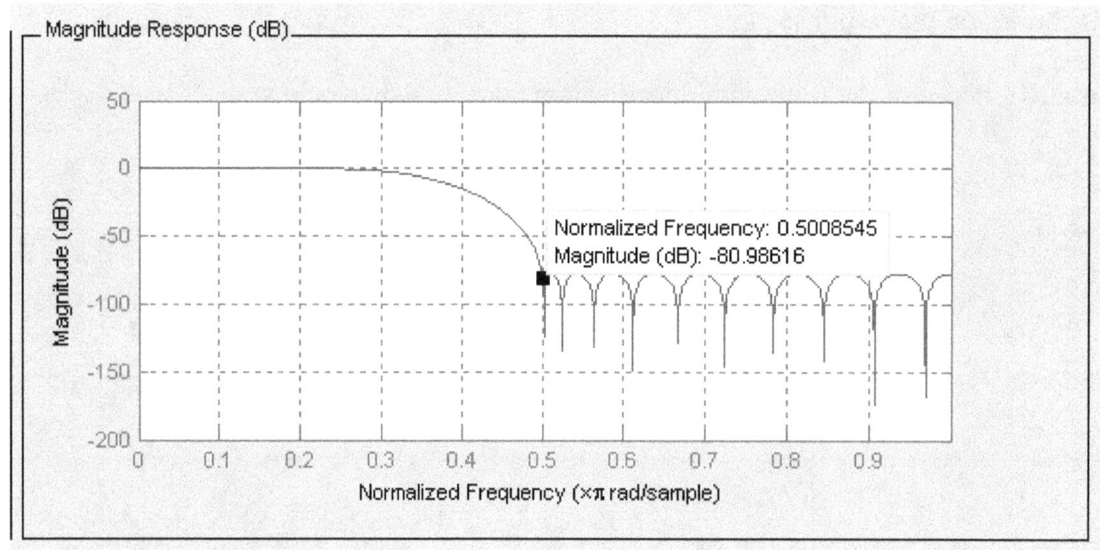

Optimizing the Design

To minimize the cost of implementation of the filter, we will try to reduce the number of coefficients by using **Minimum Order** option in the design panel.

Change the selection in **Filter Order** to **Minimum Order** in the Design Region and leave the other parameters as they are.

Click the **Design Filter** button to design the new filter.

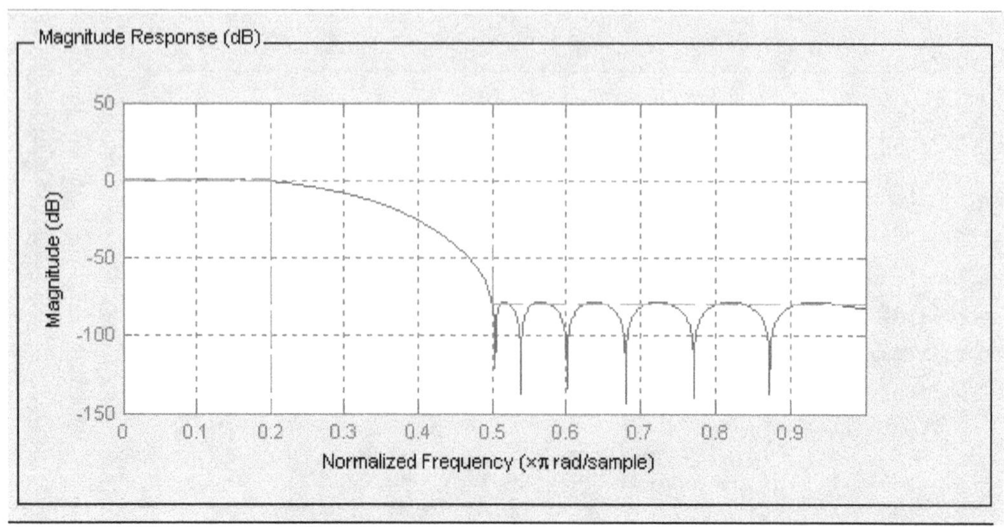

As you can see in the Current Filter Information area, the filter order decreased from 30 to 16, the number of ripples decreased and the transition width became wider. The passband and the stopband specifications still meet the design criteria.

Changing Analyses Parameters

By right-clicking on the plot and selecting Analysis Parameters, you can display a dialog box for changing analysis-specific parameters. (You can also select Analysis Parameters from the Analysis menu.)

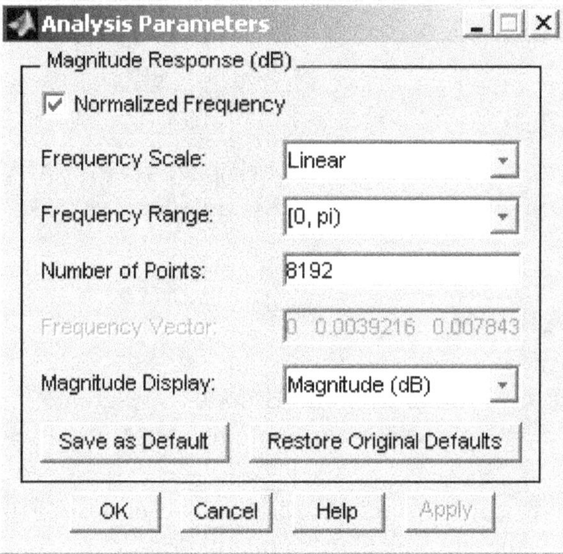

To save the displayed parameters as the default values, click **Save as Default**. To restore the MATLAB-defined default values, click **Restore Original Defaults**.

Exporting the Filter

Once you are satisfied with your design, you can export your filter to the following destinations:

- MATLAB workspace
- MAT-file
- Text-file

Select **Export** from the **File** menu.

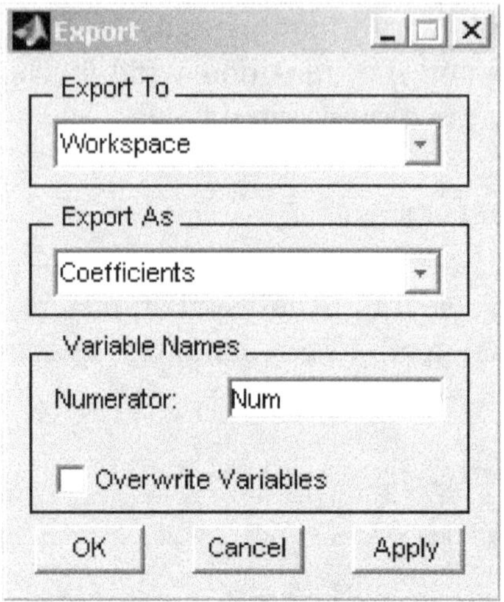

When you choose to export to the MATLAB workspace or to a MAT-file, you can export the filter as coefficients. If a DSP System Toolbox™ is available you can also export your filter as a System object.

Generating a MATLAB File

Filter Designer allows you to generate MATLAB code to re-create your filter. This enables you to embed your design into existing code or automate the creation of your filters in a script.

Select **Generate MATLAB code** from the **File** menu, choose **Filter Design Function** and specify the filename in the Generate MATLAB code dialog box.

The following code was generated from the minimum order filter we designed above:

```
function B = minorderlowfir
%MINORDERLOWFIR Returns discrete-time filter coefficients.

% MATLAB Code
% Generated by MATLAB(R) 8.1 and the Signal Processing Toolbox 6.19.
% Generated on: 11-Oct-2012 12:19:05

% Equiripple Lowpass filter designed using the FIRPM function.

% All frequency values are normalized to 1.

Fpass = 0.2;               % Passband Frequency
Fstop = 0.5;               % Stopband Frequency
Dpass = 0.057501127785;    % Passband Ripple
Dstop = 0.0001;            % Stopband Attenuation
dens  = 20;                % Density Factor

% Calculate the order from the parameters using FIRPMORD.
[N, Fo, Ao, W] = firpmord([Fpass, Fstop], [1 0], [Dpass, Dstop]);

% Calculate the coefficients using the FIRPM function.
B = firpm(N, Fo, Ao, W, {dens});
```

Quantizing a Filter

If you have the DSP System Toolbox™ installed, the **Set quantization parameters** panel is available on the sidebar:

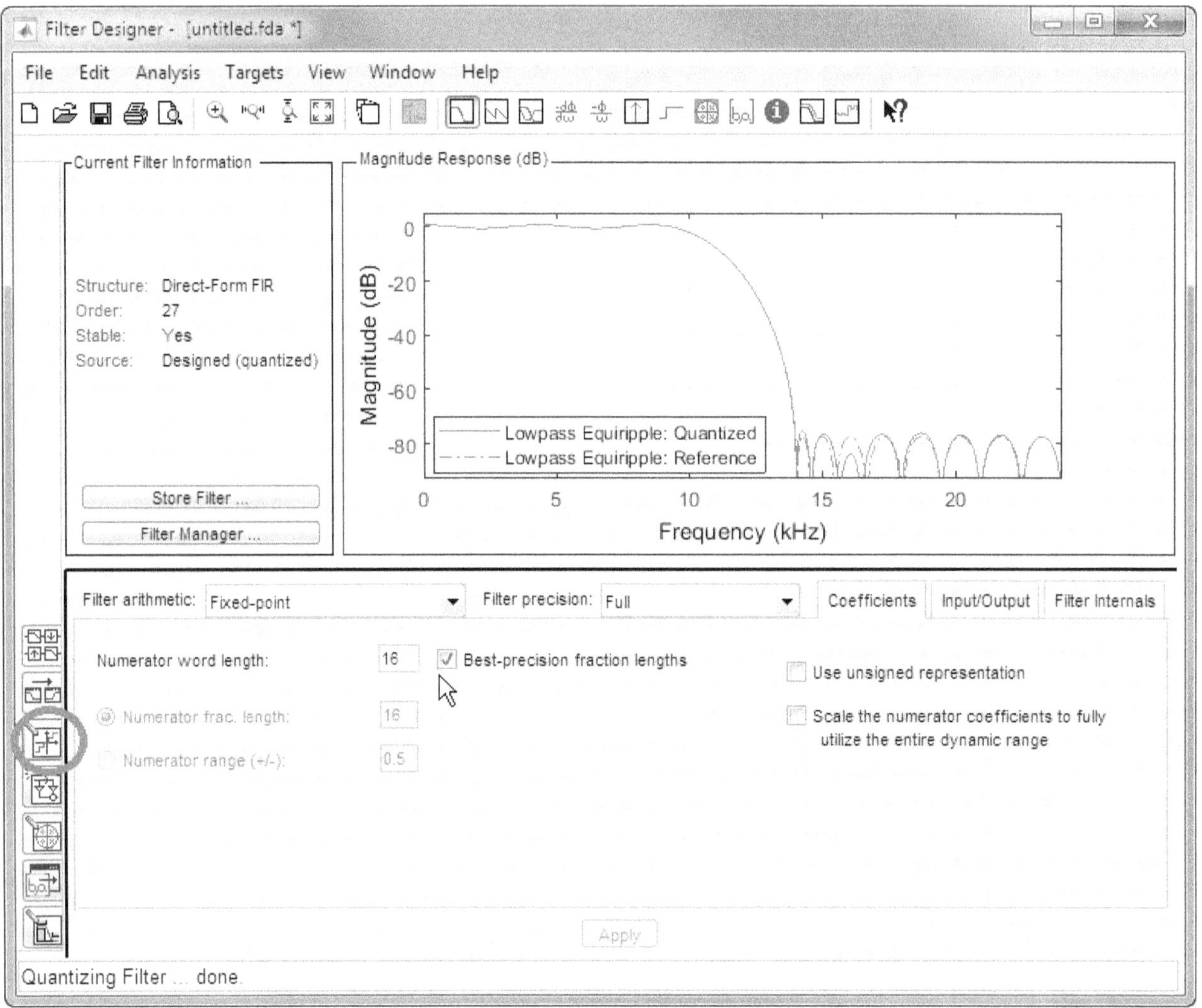

You can use this panel to quantize and analyze double-precision filters. With the DSP System Toolbox you can quantize from double-precision to single-precision. If you have the Fixed-Point Designer, you can quantize filters to fixed-point precision. Note that you cannot mix floating-point and fixed-point arithmetic in your filter.

Targets

The **Targets** menu of Filter Designer allows you to generate various types of code representing your filter. For example, you can generate C header files, XILINX coefficients(COE) files (with the DSP System Toolbox) and VHDL, Verilog along with test benches (with Filter Design HDL Coder™).

Additional Features

Filter Designer also integrates additional functionality from these other MathWorks™ products:

- **DSP System Toolbox**- Adds advanced FIR and IIR design techniques (i.e. Filter transformations, Multirate filters) and generates equivalent block for the filter
- **Embedded Coder™**- Generates, builds and deploys code for Texas Instruments C6000 processors.
- **Filter Design HDL Coder**- Generates synthesizable VHDL or Verilog code for fixed-point filters
- **Simulink®**- Generates filters from atomic Simulink blocks

4.2 Filter design using filter builder

Problem-11: Use MATLAB to generate coefficients of simple FIR filters for the following specifications.

- ➢ *8 KHz Sampling Frequency*
- ➢ *Passband from 0 to 1 KHz*
- ➢ *Stopband from 2 to 4 KHz*
- ➢ *1 dB Passband Ripple*
- ➢ *Approximately 0 dB passband attenuation*
- ➢ *Approximately -40 dB stopband attenuation*

Also test the filter with two sinusoidal signal containing 500Hz and 3000Hz frequencies respectively.

We are going to be using a graphical tool from the signal processing toolbox called "filterbuilder". Or Open Matlab and type the following command:

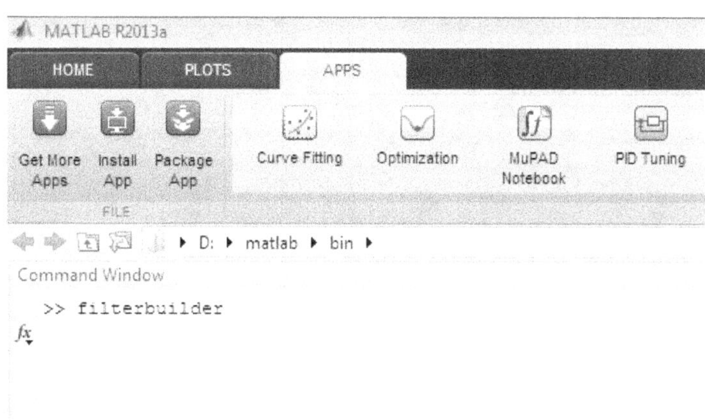

You should see the following GUI:

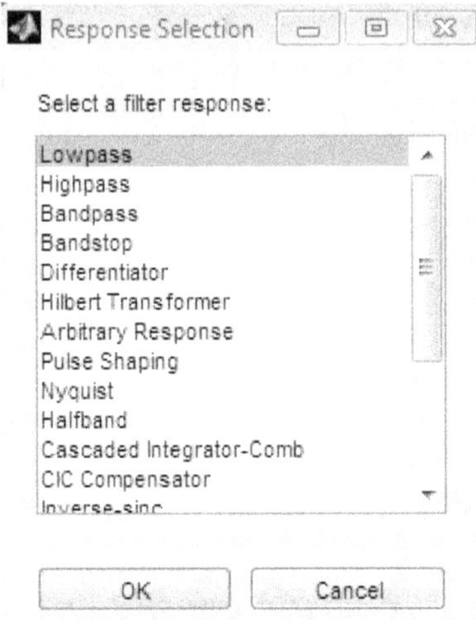

Here we select the type of filter that we would like to design. For the purpose of this example we will go ahead and choose **Lowpass**. Press **OK** once you have selected your filter type.

You will be shown another window. For a lowpass filter it should look like the following:

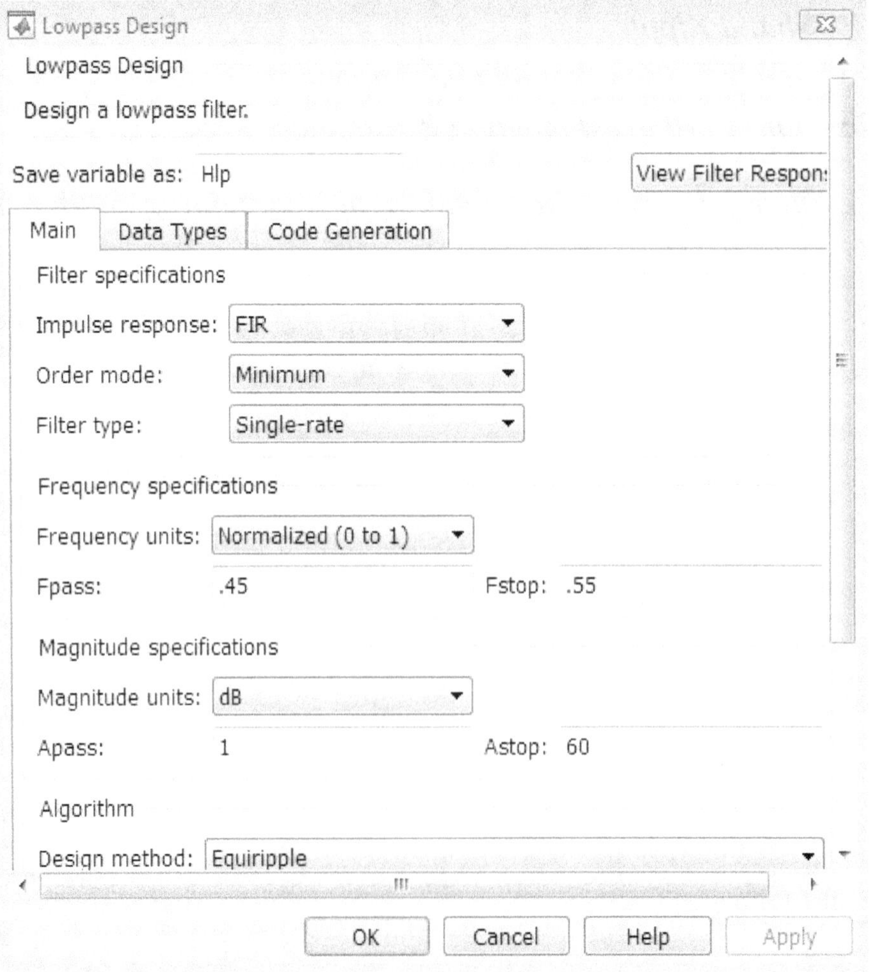

The following changes need to be made:

- ➤ **Frequency units:** Since we are processing sound, we set this value to Hz.
- ➤ **Input Fs:** This is the sample rate. For this example we use the value 8000.
- ➤ **Fpass:** This is the right edge of your passband. we use 1000 for this example.
- ➤ **Fstop:** This is the left edge of your stopband. we use 2000 for this example.
- ➤ **Apass:** Passband Attenuation – This is the tolerable amount of ripple centered about 0 allowed in the passband. For this example we use 1 dB.
- ➤ **Astop:** Stopband Attenuation – This is the upper limit of the stop band attenuation

After all of the listed changes, the window should now look like the following:

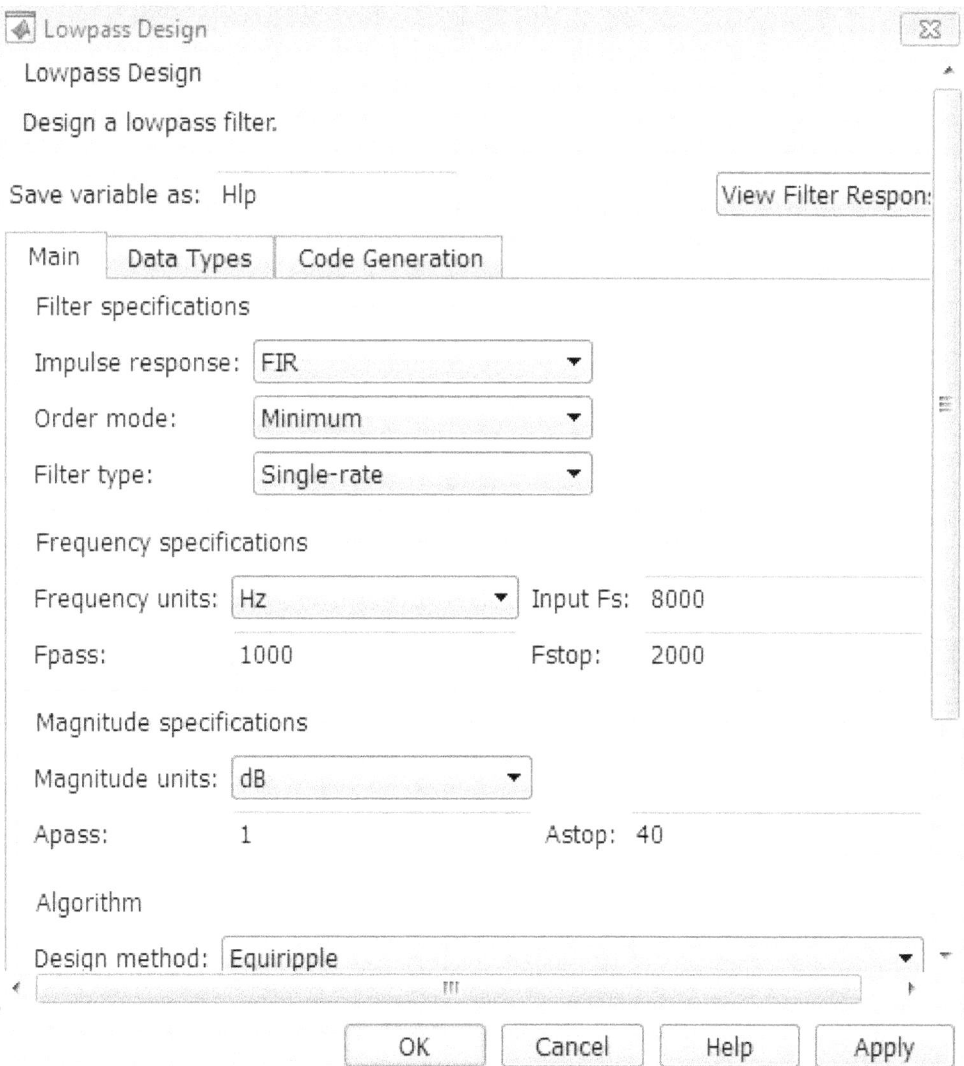

Ensure you click "Apply" in the bottom right corner after you make these changes in order to update the filter.

In order to check that we have the correct filter, we can now view its frequency response. Click the button in the top right of this window that says "View Filter Response"

My filter looks like this:

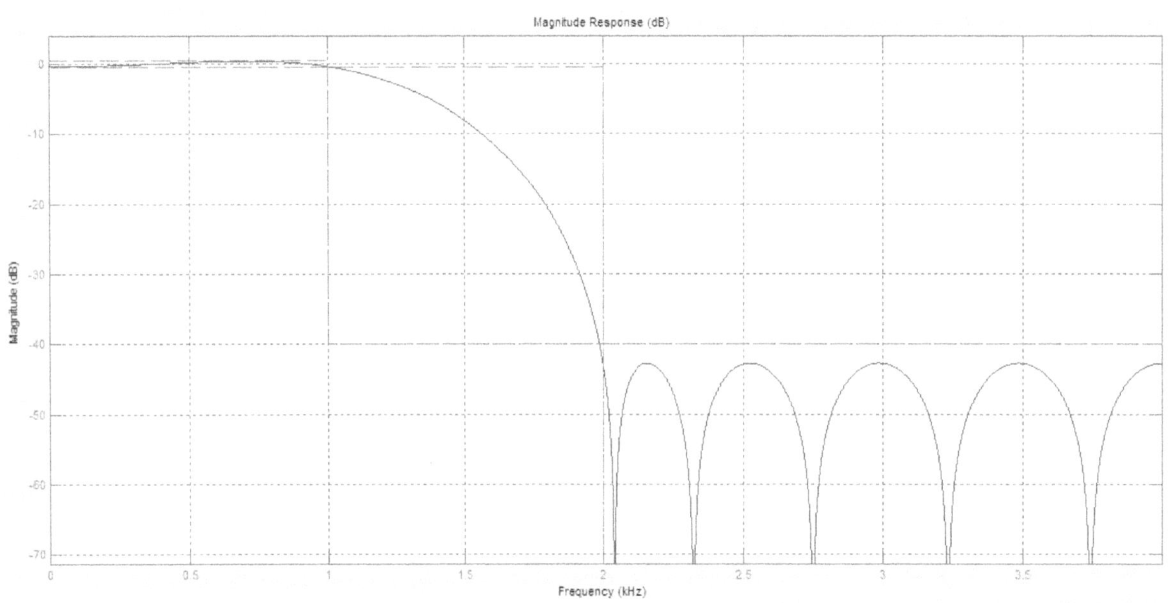

We see that this filter meets all of the required specifications.

Now, we need to get our filter coefficients.

When you hit "Apply" previously you should have gotten the following message in the Matlab terminal:

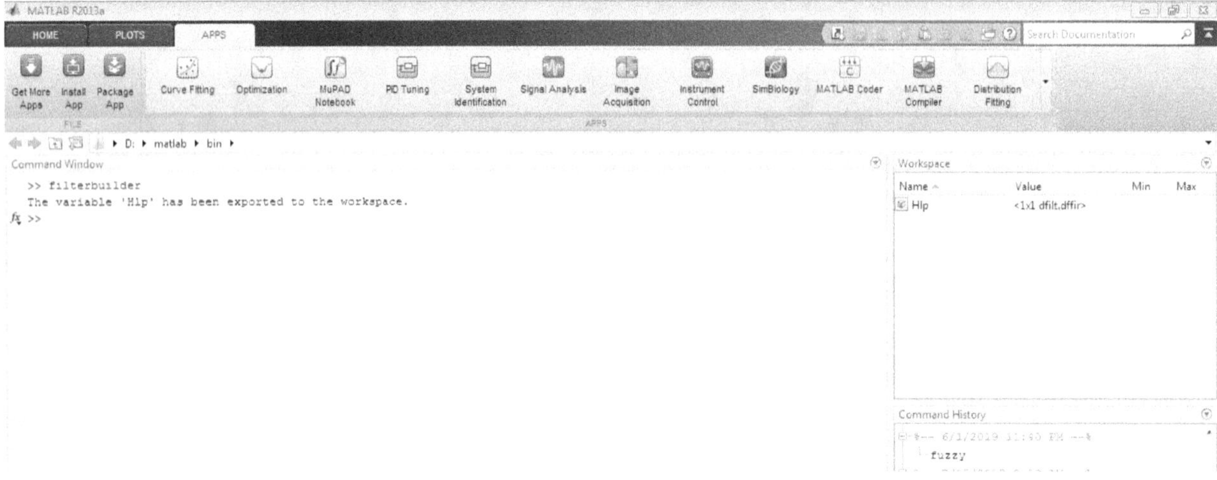

This created an object saved as Hlp (if you did not rename it).

To extract our coefficients we could run the following code:

```
>> myFilterCoeffs=Hlp.Numerator;
fx >>
```

Now if we check what the value of myFilterCoeffs…

```
>> myFilterCoeffs

myFilterCoeffs =

  Columns 1 through 12

    0.0100    0.0038   -0.0280   -0.0585   -0.0220    0.1132    0.2813    0.3583    0.2813    0.1132   -0.0220   -0.0585

  Columns 13 through 15

   -0.0280    0.0038    0.0100

fx >>
```

There are our 16 coefficients!

Testing the filter:

Let's create two sinusoids and filter them with our shiny new filter!

The following code creates 100 samples of 2 sinusoids with frequencies of 500 and 3000 at a sample rate of 8000.

```
>> t=1:100;

>> plot(data1,t)
>> data1=sin(2*pi*t*500/8000);
>> data2=sin(2*pi*t*3000/8000);
>>
```

Convince yourself that these are actually sinusoids by plotting them.

Here I plot 100 samples of our 500Hz sinusoid. I use the following code:

```
>> plot(data1)
fx >>
```

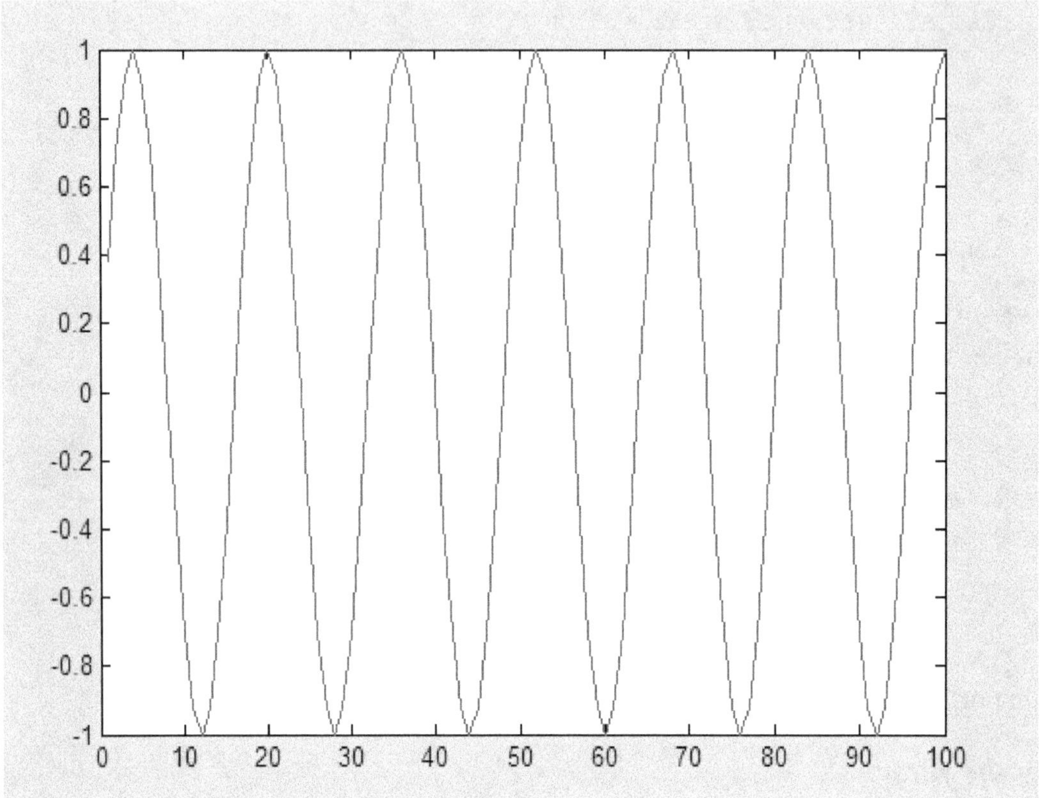

Here I plot 100 samples of our 3000Hz sinusoid. I use the following code:

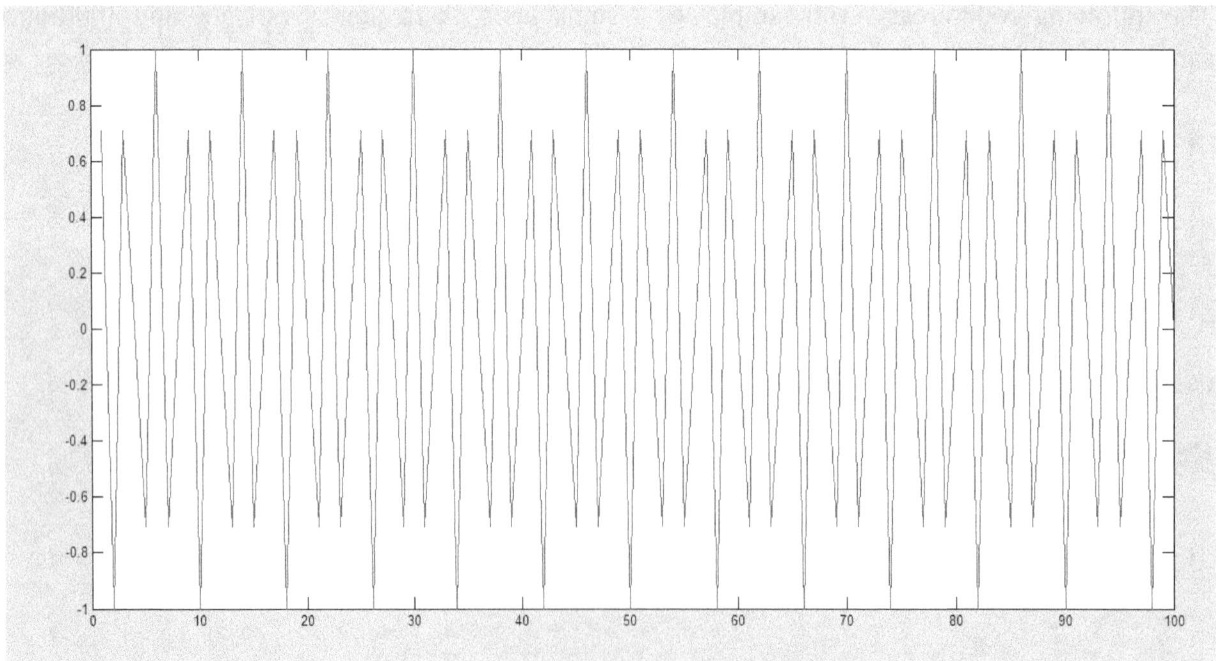

We see the variables in our workspace have upper and lower limits of 1 and -1 respectively. This is exactly what we expect considering these are plain sinusoids.

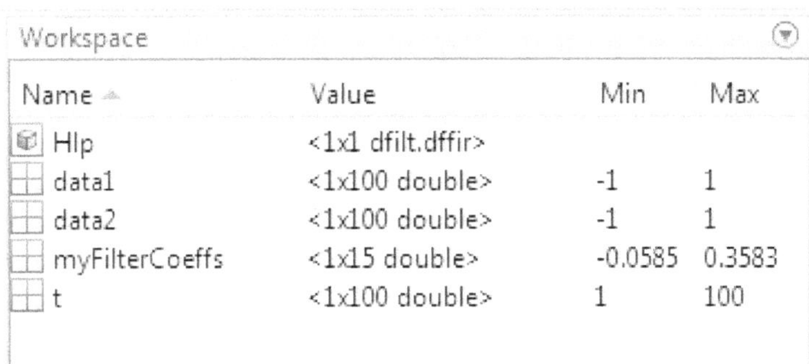

Using the filter command we can pass our data and our filter object called Hlp(unless you renamed it) and obtain filtered data.

So after running the following code:

```
>> data1filt=filter(Hlp,data1);
>> data2filt=filter(Hlp,data2);
>>
```

We see the following in our workspace:

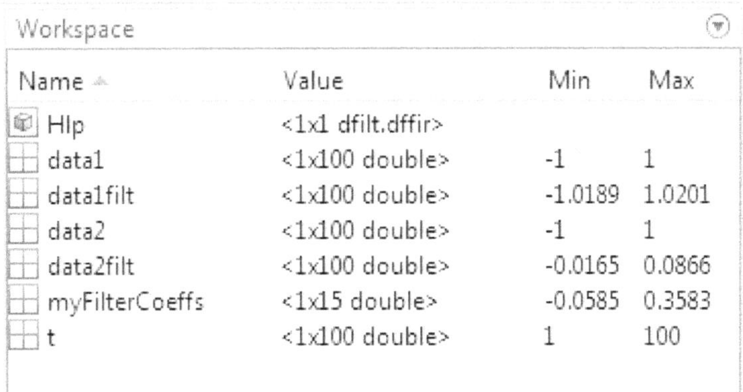

Plot the data1filt

Plot(data1filt)

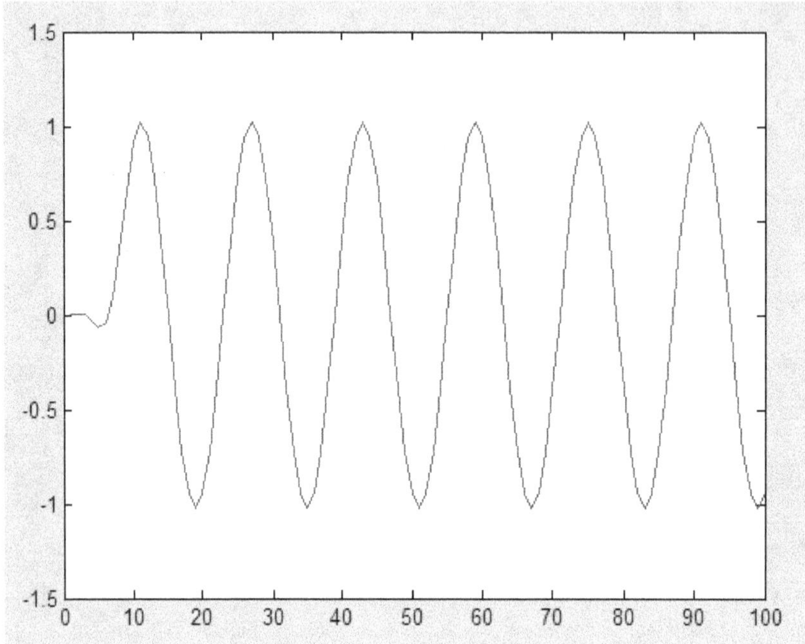

Plot the data2filt

plot(data2filt)

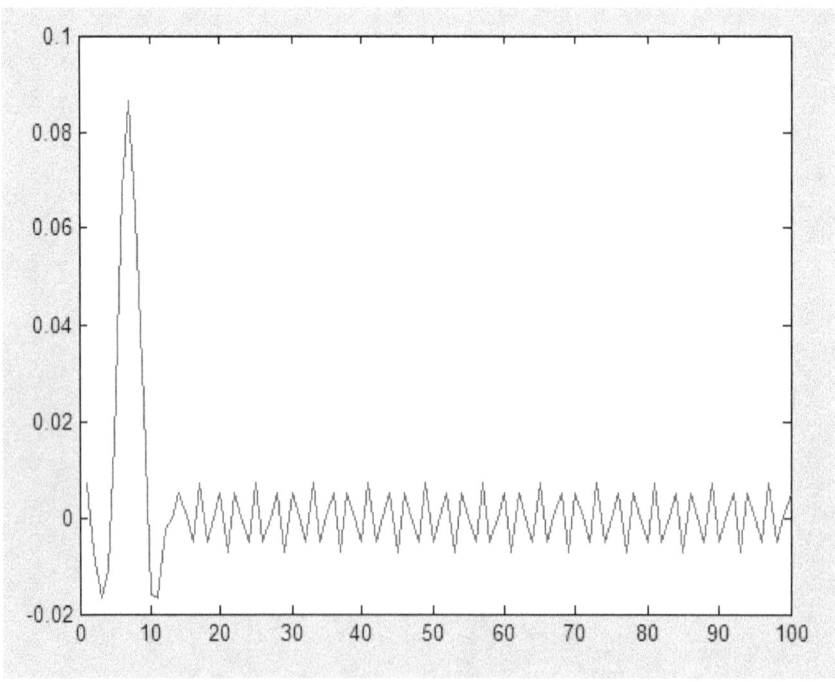

We see that our 500Hz sinusoid is attenuated only slightly but the 3000 Hz sinusoid is attenuated dramatically! This is exactly how our filter should behave.